"In *Choreographing Dirt*, Angenette Spalink excavates and activates our intimate and interwoven dance with the material stuff of the earth – call it dirt, soil, detritus, mud, peat, humus, ash – it is the delicate and constant dance partner of our intractably embodied lives. In light of current myriad crises, *Choreographing Dirt* analyzes how performance – dance, theatre and cultural enactment – can trace the impacts of extraction and trade, reveal displacement and destruction of human and more-than-human lives, unearth and lay bare racist and genocidal histories long buried in soil, or celebrate deeply rooted cultural reciprocities with the land around us. *Choreographing Dirt* is a lucid and compelling analysis of the essential work of the performing arts in the era of climate change: to illuminate and complicate human kinship with the more-than-human world. Spalink has made an elegant and incisive contribution to the intersectional fields of ecodramaturgy, performance studies, dance studies and environmental humanities."

Theresa J. May, author of *Earth Matters on Stage: Ecology, Environment and American Theatre*

"Spalink does the urgent work of bringing ecocriticism to dance studies, taking seriously how dirt is choreographed on the stage, as well as how dirt in turn choreographs the movement of others in and across biological, geographical, and cultural spaces. Her analyses of theater and dance pieces in which dirt takes center stage model how the movements of dirt itself offer new insights to intractable ecological problems."

Rosemary Candelario, University of Texas at Austin

"By attending to the ways in which the 'choreography of matter matters,' *Choreographing Dirt* represents a welcome and much-needed expansion of ecocriticism and ecodramaturgy into the fields of movement and dance. Focusing on well-chosen case studies, Spalink's analysis astutely reveals how performance can illuminate connections between the displacement of resources and environmental injustices."

Dr. Wendy Arons, Professor of Drama and Director of the Center for the Arts in Society, Carnegie Mellon University

Choreographing Dirt

This book is an innovative study that places performance and dance studies in conversation with ecology by exploring the significance of dirt in performance.

Focusing on a range of 20th- and 21st-century performances that include modern dance, dance-theatre, Butoh, and everyday life, this book demonstrates how the choreography of dirt makes biological, geographical, and cultural meaning, what the author terms "biogeocultography." Whether it's the Foundling Father digging into the earth's strata in Suzan-Lori Park's *The America Play* (1994), peat hurling through the air in Pina Bausch's *The Rite of Spring* (1975), dancers frantically shovelling out fistfuls of dirt in Eveoke Dance Theatre's *Las Mariposas* (2010), or Butoh performers dancing with fungi in Iván-Daniel Espinosa's *Messengers Divinos* (2018), each example shows how the incorporation of dirt can reveal micro-level interactions between species – like the interplay between microscopic skin bacteria and soil protozoa – and macro-level interactions – like the transformation of peat to a greenhouse gas. By demonstrating the stakes of moving dirt, this book posits that performance can operate as a space to grapple with the multifaceted ecological dilemmas of the Anthropocene.

This book will be of broad interest to both practitioners and researchers in theatre, performance studies, dance, ecocriticism, and the environmental humanities.

Angenette Spalink is an Assistant Professor of Performance Studies at Texas A&M University.

Routledge Studies in Theatre, Ecology, and Performance

Studies in Theatre, Ecology, and Performance (STEP) explores intersections between theatre, ecology, and performance studies in a global context. Amidst the current pandemic, the threat of environmental degradation—in particular climate change, challenges to clean water and air, food insecurity, and species extinction—seems to lurk just off stage. Yet, ecology and the environment remain overriding concerns of the Anthropocene and the pandemic is incriminated in received interspecies practice. Theatre and performance studies can add unique contributions to current conversations around future human behaviours. STEP seeks proposals from those working in intersecting fields of theatre, performance studies, and ecology across the globe. Ecology can be defined as the study of organisms and their interactive environment or "home."

The Stage Lives of Animals
Zooesis and Performance
Una Chaudhuri

Earth Matters on Stage
Ecology and Environment in American Theater
Theresa J. May

Choreographing Dirt
Movement, Performance, and Ecology in the Anthropocene
Angenette Spalink

For more information on the series please visit the series page: *https://www.routledge.com/Routledge-Studies-in-Theatre-Ecology-and-Performance/book-series/STEP#*

Choreographing Dirt
Movement, Performance, and Ecology in the Anthropocene

Angenette Spalink

LONDON AND NEW YORK

First published 2024
by Routledge
4 Park Square, Milton Park, Abingdon, Oxon OX14 4RN

and by Routledge
605 Third Avenue, New York, NY 10158

Routledge is an imprint of the Taylor & Francis Group, an informa business.

© 2024 Angenette Spalink

The right of Angenette Spalink to be identified as author of this work has been asserted in accordance with sections 77 and 78 of the Copyright, Designs and Patents Act 1988.

All rights reserved. No part of this book may be reprinted or reproduced or utilised in any form or by any electronic, mechanical, or other means, now known or hereafter invented, including photocopying and recording, or in any information storage or retrieval system, without permission in writing from the publishers.

Trademark notice: Product or corporate names may be trademarks or registered trademarks, and are used only for identification and explanation without intent to infringe.

British Library Cataloguing-in-Publication Data
A catalogue record for this book is available from the British Library

ISBN: 9780367758400 (hbk)
ISBN: 9780367758431 (pbk)
ISBN: 9781003164234 (ebk)

DOI: 10.4324/9781003164234

Typeset in Times New Roman
by KnowledgeWorks Global Ltd.

For Daniel and Francesca Paeonia

Contents

List of figures   *x*
Acknowledgments   *xi*

Introduction: Biogeocultography   1

1 Performative Taphonomy: Excavating and Exhuming the Past in Suzan-Lori Parks's *The America Play*   23

2 Staging Extraction: Peat's Vitality in Pina Bausch's *The Rite of Spring*   42

3 A Dirty *Pas De Deux:* Dirt, Skin, and "Transcorporeality" in Eveoke Dance Theatre's *Las Mariposas*   58

4 Mycelium in Motion: Choreographing Care in Iván-Daniel Espinosa's *Messengers Divinos*   78

Conclusion: Moving with the Trouble   96

Index   *101*

Figures

3.1 Nikki Dunnan as Dedé Mirabal, ensemble dancers Becky Hurt, Molly Terbovich-Ridenhour, Bruce Walker, and Shayna Cribbs, and Charlene Penner as the Butterfly in the scene "Unearthing the Girls" from the performance at the Gran Teatro del Cibao in Santiago, Dominican Republic, Tuesday, November 29, 2011. Photo by Tim Botsko. 61
3.2 In "The Cemetery is Beginning to Flower," (the scene following the murder) dirt coats the stage and many of the dancers. Photo by Tim Botsko. 62
3.3 Nikki Dunnan as Dedé Mirabal dancing in a bin of dirt. From the performance at the Centro Cultural Mauricio Baez in Santo Domingo, Dominican Republic, Thursday December 1, 2011. Photo by Tim Botsko. 67
3.4 In "The Cemetery is Beginning to Flower," the ensemble members partner with the dirt and the young sisters perform a dance with the clothing of their older counterparts now buried in the bins. Centro Cultural Mauricio Baez in Santo Domingo, Dominican Republic, Thursday December 1, 2011. Photo by Tim Botsko. 72
4.1 Dancers and fungi performing in *Messengers Divinos* (2018) at the Seattle International Butoh Festival. Photo by Jim Lee Carey. 79
4.2 Fungi, dirt, and dancers in *Messengers Divinos* (2018) at the Seattle International Butoh Festival. Photo by Jim Lee Carey. 81
4.3 A dancer consuming fungi in *Messengers Divinos* (2018) at the Seattle International Butoh Festival. Photo by Jim Lee Carey. 91

Acknowledgments

During this project, I had a baby. Three months later there was a global pandemic. Caring for and attempting to keep a newborn safe in the early stages of the pandemic was overwhelming to say the least. I am deeply indebted to my parents, Annette and Jim Stacer, who put their lives on hold to help us during this period, providing childcare so we could continue working. Thank you, so much.

The seeds of this book developed in the muddy intersections of graduate school, botanical fieldwork, and dance classes. Deep gratitude goes to many people for their contributions, support, and encouragement. First and foremost, I would like to thank Daniel, who has always been a source of love, compassion, encouragement, and unwavering support. This book and the adventures that inspired it would not have been possible without you. I would also like to thank Frankie, whose birth was a real game changer. You amaze me and make me laugh every day.

I am profoundly grateful to faculty and friends in the Department of Theatre and Film at Bowling Green State University, where this project began. Thank you to my advisors Scott Magelssen and Jonathan Chambers for your enthusiasm and impact on my scholarship. You both always supported my work with dirt, and I am deeply grateful. Thank you also to Lesa Lockford and Margaret Yacobucci for your feedback and ideas. Deep thanks to the incredible community at BGSU for your thoughtful conversations and lasting friendships: Sara Chambers, Quincy Thomas, Heidi Nees-Carver, Miriam Hahn-Thomas, Patrick Konesko, Alyssa Konesko, Slade Billew, Darin Kerr, Cynthia Baron, Elizabeth Guthrie, Matthew Nicosia, Michelle Cowin Gibbs, Chanelle Vigue, JP Staszel, and Alexis Riley.

Profound thanks to my writing group. The ideas in this book have developed substantially from your feedback and suggestions: Lisa Woynarski, Jonah Winn-Lenetsky, Kelli Shermeyer, and especially Courtney Ryan for being my Zoom writing companion. I am also grateful to the Ecology & Performance Working Group at ASTR which was a generative space to develop my research. Thank you to Katie Schaag, Malin Palani, Clara Margaret Wilch,

Liz Ivkovich, Antonia Krueger, and Ashley Chang, for the many fruitful and exciting conversations.

Thank you to my colleagues in Performance Studies at Texas A&M University for your support and contributions to this project: James R. Ball III, Kim Kattari, Leonardo Cardoso, Matthew Delciampo, David Donkor, Donnalee Dox, Martin Regan, Jesse O'Rear, Cory LaFevers, Daniel Humphrey, and Zachary Price.

I am grateful for the dissertation fellowship I received during my graduate studies at Bowling Green State University where many of these ideas developed. I would also like to thank the Performance Studies program at Texas A&M University for financial research assistance. Thanks also to the Academy for Visual and Performing Arts at Texas A&M University for grants that supported my research.

Thank you to the artists who generously allowed me to access their work as well as those who allowed Evangeline Rose Whitlock or me to interview them: Anastasia Wilson, James Ogden, Charlene Penner, Nikki Dunnan, Araceli Carrera, Jessica Rabanzo-Flores, Erika Malone, Becky Hurt, Shayna Cribbs, Molly Terbovich-Ridenhour, Bruce Walker, Ericka Aisha Moore, Catherine Kineavy, Jack Lampl, David Atchison, Sue Dye, Suz Knight, Sarah Karpicus, Andy Lowe, and Iván-Daniel Espinosa. I am also incredibly thankful to the botanists who let me accompany them on their fieldwork, specifically Ernie Schuyler, Tom Rawinski, and Gary Fleming.

Deep gratitude to Evangeline Rose Whitlock, my collaborator and co-presenter at the *Earth Matters on Stage* Conference (2012). Thank you also to Shayna Ambers and Zachary Sheldon for your fantastic transcriptions.

Immense thanks to Routledge editors Laura Hussey and Swatti Hindwan, series editor Sarah Standing, and the entire Routledge production team.

Finally, a heartfelt thanks to friends and family, near and far, for your inspiration, support, and love: Lauren Urbanek, Lydia Bragg, Denisse Guerrero-Harvey, Brian Harvey, Katie Freker, Sam Vevang, Teresa Daining, Justin Daining, Ameera Nimjee, Jimmy Stacer, Ruth Spalink, Larry Spalink, Jolena Spalink, Annaliese Spalink, Jonathan Spalink, Christy Spalink, Ben Spalink, Robin Globus Veldman, and Meredith Wells. Special thanks to Lyn Pilch and Dance Fabulous for creating much-needed dance spaces and reminding me that dance is crucial.

An earlier version of Chapter 1 was published in *Modern Drama* 60.1 (2017): 69–88 and is republished here with permission. An earlier version of Chapter 3 was published in *Theatre Annual* 68 (2015): 1–21 and is republished here with permission.

Introduction
Biogeocultography

Approximately fifty black bags, stacked about a meter high, line the side of a winding dirt road. The bags, chockfull of dirt, are snugly aligned in a haphazard row. They gleam in the sunshine as the light's reflection makes them appear bright and shiny. The mise-en-scéne is that of a rural country road. The presence of the glossy black bags is a sharp contrast to the dirt, dried grass, and conifers that surround them. The same bags appear in a different location; this time there are thousands of them. Some of them are in disorganized heaps and others are lined in long organized rows stacked five layers high. Flatbed trucks and cranes convert the chaos into order, transferring the bags from the jumbled piles into systematized rows.[1] These are only two of the thousands of sites across Fukushima Prefecture where bags of dirt are being collected, transferred, and stored. The bags all contain radioactive dirt from the Fukushima nuclear disaster.

On March 11, 2011, a 9.1 magnitude earthquake triggered a tsunami that wreaked devasting damage on the Fukushima Daiichi Nuclear Power Plant in Ōkuma, Fukushima, Japan.[2] This resulted in the release of radioactive materials – Xenon 133, Iodine 131, Cesium 134, and Cesium 137 – into the atmosphere, local water sources, the Pacific Ocean, and the soil (Yasunari et al. 2011; Ohnuma and Ishii 2019; Hashimoto et al. 2022).[3] Following the disaster, part of the decontamination process involved removing the now radioactive soil. The Japanese government hired contractors to clear out the contaminated soil, transferring it into black bags. These bags soon became ubiquitous, visibly piling up and blanketing Fukushima Prefecture's landscape. As the quantity and volume of the bags surged, it became apparent that these bags of dirt would need to be relocated. Eventually, many of them were moved to interim storage facilities in Fukushima. In 2015, *The Mainichi* reported that approximately 9.16 million bags of dirt were being stored at 114,700 facilities across Fukushima Prefecture (2015). In 2022, *The Asahi Shimbun* reported that dirt was still being temporarily housed in 830 locations in Fukushima Prefecture, elucidating that "the volume of contaminated soil and other radioactive materials awaiting shipment totals 8,460 cubic meters, which is the equivalent of 130 trucks each weighing 10 tons" (2022). Even now, eleven years after the

DOI: 10.4324/9781003164234-1

disaster, the bags' destination has yet to be determined. Japan's government has pledged that the contaminated dirt will be moved outside of Fukushima Prefecture by 2045 (McCurry 2019). In the meantime, it still resides within the temporary Fukushima facilities.

The soil's relocation from its habitat to the bags and the bags' transfer to interim storage facilities and subsequent organization within the facilities are all sequences of movement that can be understood as choreography – the structuring or ordering of movement. As dance scholar Susan Leigh Foster attests, "choreography can stipulate both the kinds of actions performed and their sequence or progression" (2011, 2). The movement of the bags of dirt, which traverse biological, geographical, and cultural boundaries, enacts what I call a biological/geographical/cultural choreography, hereafter shortened to the neologism *biogeocultography*.

Biogeocultography is the structured movement of ecological matter through geographic, biological, and cultural spaces. Movement through these spaces can be planned and deliberate. For example, collecting, pressing, drying a daffodil, and then affixing it to a sheet of paper is a deliberate biogeocultography. The daffodil is geographically moved from the soil, pressed between a stack of books, and then moved to a piece of paper. Through this locomotion the daffodil dies and is transformed from an ecologically active entity to a piece of art or archival specimen. Not all biogeocultographies are intentional though, as the movement of ecological matter through one space (e.g., geographic space and cultural space) can cause parallel but inadvertent movements through the other spaces. For instance, sequences of movements that geographically displace soil are the impetus for the biological and cultural transformation of soil to dirt. Scientifically soil becomes dirt when it is removed from the site of its original geographic location and therefore no longer retains its historical and broader ecological context. As biogeochemist Patrick Megonigal succinctly puts it, "dirt is displaced soil" (Raloff 2008). The *geographical* displacement of soil from its ecological context alters it, both compositionally and culturally. *Biologically*, the soil's dislocation changes how it processes and releases carbon dioxide and leads to the eventual cessation of decompositional processes within it (Birge et al. 2015). *Culturally*, the displacement of soil transforms it from a biologically diverse and chemically dynamic element to dirt, an abject object out of place that transgresses boundaries (Kristeva 1982; Douglas 1966). The interactions of these geographical, biological, and cultural dynamics resulting from the movement of soil are a *biogeocultography*, a process through which the soil becomes dirt.

The *biogeocultography* of the bags of Fukushima dirt transforms how it is perceived and understood. The soil becomes dirt through the movements that *geographically* displace it. The dirt's *biology* is transformed through radioactive materials, the effects of which are multi-scalar. Its biological composition is also altered through its dislocation, changing its chemistry and decomposition processes. The sequence of movements through which the bags are transferred to temporary facilities causes the soil to become *culturally* constructed as dirt – an abject entity that disturbs organized systems. Through its initial removal and organization within the facilities, the government attempts to restore order. Nevertheless, the effort is ultimately infelicitous as the dirt cannot be stored there permanently. The dirt must be moved, but it has nowhere to go.

Importantly, the bags of dirt are not solo performers in this choreography. Rather, their movements through geographical, biological, and cultural spaces also structure the movements of other bodies and ecological matter. Because the dirt is radioactive, Japan's Ministry of the Environment issued strict procedures for its handling and storage (2015, 2018). Workers at decontamination sites donned protective masks, hats, gloves, and suits and storage sites were subject to detailed protocols. Here, biogeocultography not only exposes choreography as critical to the biological, geographical, and cultural construction of dirt, but in the specific case of the Fukushima dirt, it reveals that the dirt's movements were activated through its toxicity, which made it undesirable. The dirt's movement was an attempt to dispose of it, an effort to restore biological, geographic, and cultural order. This choreography of displacement cannot restore order, though, because the dirt contains invisible but measurable materials that can radically transform human and more-than-human bodies.[4] The biogeocultography of the bags of Fukushima dirt exposes the intricate entanglements of movement, materiality, and ecology.

While the biogeocultography of the Fukushima dirt is not performance in a "traditional" sense, it aligns with theatre scholar Carl Lavery's characterization of performance as something no longer bound to a "conventional" stage. He describes performance as an embodied medium that "does" something, it is the "distribution of organic and inorganic bodies in actual time that creates sensations and experiences in the here and now" (Lavery 2019, 2). The existence and movement of the bags in time and space "does" something: it affects the experiences of people and things in its proximity and, to a greater extent, alters biological, geographic, and cultural understandings of the soil's materiality and function.

I begin this book with the biogeocultography of the Fukushima dirt because it illustrates two points that are crucial to *Choreographing Dirt*. First, the choreography of dirt (and other ecological matter) matters, both in and of itself but also because it structures the movements of other bodies and materials. Second, analyzing the movement of dirt through the lens of choreography offers a different perspective of the relationship between ecology[5] and performance/dance. It demonstrates that not only is choreography critical to the biological, geographic, and cultural meaning of dirt, but when placed on stage – as in the case studies in this book – these meanings are actualized, and the dirt performs. *Choreographing Dirt* argues that the choreography of dirt constructs meaning not only within dance and performance studies but also within natural science.

4 *Introduction*

While this book focuses on performance in the more "traditional" sense, in each case study, I argue that – like the Fukushima dirt – the composition and movement of the human and more-than-human bodies on stage (and page) "does" something. Focusing on 20th- and 21st-century dramatic text and performances that occur across a range of geographies in North America, Central America, and Europe, I analyze diverse entanglements of materiality and movement where literal dirt, peat, and fungi are vital choreographic elements. Through analyses of Suzan Lori Parks's *The America Play* (1994), Pina Bausch's *The Rite of Spring* (1975), Eveoke Dance Theatre's *Las Mariposas* (2010), and Iván-Daniel Espinosa's Butoh dance piece *Messengers Divinos: A Meditation on Time, Space, Corporeality, & Consciousness* (2018), I argue that seemingly innocuous ecological interactions among humans and ecological matter (e.g., dirt, peat, fungi) challenge anthropocentric frameworks by revealing that the performer is not always human, and that these biogeocultographies construct meaning. These case studies also demonstrate the ways in which performance and the practices of everyday life are not discreetly bounded; rather they are permeable and high stakes, as the radioactive Fukushima dirt, the Covid-19 pandemic, and the myriad social and environmental dilemmas of the Anthropocene make abundantly clear.

Dirt

My interest in the intersections of ecology, movement, and performance was bolstered by summers of tromping through swamps and bogs, and hiking through woods and flood plains, accompanying my partner on his botanical fieldwork. During these excursions, I joined botanists in hot pursuit of Cyperaceae, a family of grass-like plants. As a result, I found myself covered in dirt, soaked with sweat, swarmed by bugs, and un-showered. These moments expanded my understanding of the body's porosity, of my embodied relationship with the landscape, and of the performance[6] of "nature."[7] One experience that stands out: I was trudging through a swamp in Virginia and my boots kept getting stuck in the deep mud to the point that it made it challenging to walk. When I commented on this, one of the local botanists said, "Oh we have a name for that; it's called the bog-step two-step." When you take one step forward, your boot gets stuck in the substrate and when you try to pull it out you fall back two steps. As a scholar and dancer, this gave me a new framework for considering movement.[8] This shift from the studio to the swamp made me contemplate how the consistency and texture of the terrain affected my body's ability to move. These experiences challenged my understanding of embodiment and its relation to different landscapes. Feeling the buildup of dirt, bug spray, and perspiration seeping into my skin made me contemplate the permeability of the body differently. Navigating my tired, sweaty, dirty body through difficult terrain inhabited by more-than-human beings made me

Introduction 5

come to terms with my own anthropocentric tendencies. Over the years, these material encounters have seeped into my research, teaching, and practice in varied and unexpected ways, perhaps most explicitly in my approach to this book.

Just as the dirt, mud, and terrain shaped the choreography of my movement, in *Choreographing Dirt*, I analyze text and performances where dirt functions as a critical choreographic element. Each case study is connected through the movement of dirt and the ways that dirt structures and affects the movements of other performers.[9] Dirt, a word and material loaded with cultural and biological significance, is a fundamental, perhaps overlooked component – in everyday life and performance – that is perfectly suited for ecocritical inquiry. Dirt is a fascinating element: it turns death into a vital source of life, contains thousands of different species, and retains remnants of both the ancient and recent past. It is "lively emergent, intra-acting phenomena" (Alaimo 2008, 249), which has the potential to alter perceptions of ecological exchanges in performance.

The *Oxford English Dictionary* first describes dirt (*n.*) simply as "excrement;" then, as "unclean matter, such as soils any object by adhering to it; filth; *esp.* the wet mud or mire of the ground, consisting of earth and waste matter mingled with water," and "mud; soil, earth, mould; brick-earth" (2013a). On the other hand, soil (*n.*) is defined as "the earth or ground; the face or surface of the earth" and subsequently as "a piece or stretch of ground; a place or site" and "a land or country; a region, province, or district" (2013b). While these definitions indicate that the two words are not synonyms, they do not clearly signify the specific differences between dirt and soil. So, if dirt and soil are distinct from one another, what exactly are the differences?

Soil contains abiotic elements, which, depending on its geographic location, could include rock, sand, clay, silt, and various minerals. Soil also contains biotic elements, living or dead organisms such as insects and other animals, bacteria, fungi, and plants. Biologist James B. Nardi asserts that "A staggering number of individual organisms as well as species representing all kingdoms – plants, animals, fungi, protozoa, bacteria – live in the soil" (2007, ix). In fact, one square meter of soil can contain up to 10 trillion bacteria, 10 billion protozoa (one-celled organisms), 5 million nematodes (roundworms), not to mention 170,000 other organisms, including mites, springtails, insects, myriapods, spiders, earthworms, snails, and slugs (Nardi 2007, ix). Ecologist Richard Bardgett affirms that just one cubic centimeter of arable soil can contain up to 350 different species (2005, 31). These biotic elements aid in the decay of organic matter such as dead plants and animals. Discussing the difference between soil and dirt, Megonigal explains,

> soil is the compilation of minerals, air, water, animals and other living matter (and their wastes or decaying bodies) that accumulate in layers and become compacted over time.... When particles of that soil erode or are

dug up, they lose the "history" of their place ... essentially their associations with particles that might have been above, below, and to their sides.

(Raloff 2008)

As previously discussed, soil becomes dirt, then, when it is removed from its original environment. Removing soil from its habitat alters its chemistry and ability to decompose matter (Birge et al. 2015). These modifications affect how soil releases carbon dioxide and will eventually alter the flora and fauna that reside within it (Birge et al. 2015).

Through its displacement soil biologically transforms into dirt. Culturally, however, the word dirt acquires different meanings. As discussed regarding the Fukushima dirt, soil becomes dirt when it transgresses boundaries and creates disorder (Douglas 1966). Arborist William Bryant Logan describes dirt's transuding essence, "[it's] the stuff that won't come off your collar. It's what smells in a compost heap. It's what blows around on the floor or makes the sheets feel gritty and slick" (2007, 7). Dirt is an element that surrounds humans in their day-to-day existence. It permeates boundaries by getting under fingernails, in sheets, between toes, and in food. Logan contends that "it is short, strong, and leaves a taste in the mouth ... you want to get ahold of it and chew it" (2007, 38). He alludes to the idea that there is something visceral and kinesthetic about dirt, both as a word that you distinctly feel in your mouth when you utter it and as an element you can feel squished between your toes. Likewise, feminist writer Rebecca Solnit further links humans, dirt, and earth through their linguistic origins:

> Etymology connects *humus* and *homo* in Latin; *chthon* (earth) and *epichthonios* (human) in Greek; and Adam derives from *clod* in Hebrew, as in clod of dirt. The microcosm of any dirt, all dirt, is linked to the whole of the globe by the word *earth*, by *terre* in French.
>
> (2001, 152, italics in original)

The etymologies of earth and humans are closely connected. Dirt is not only an element that is part of everyday existence, but it is also the substance from which humans, in many creation mythologies, are formed and the place to which bodies will eventually return. Bodies interred in the ground, however, do not remain dead—eventually they teem with life as fungi, larvae, and bacteria inhabit the remains. In this way soil perpetuates itself, turning death into a vital source of life as nutrients are released.

"Dirt" also conjures up distinct cultural conceptions regarding notions of "dirty" and "clean." Writer Katherine Ashenburg notes that "The archetypal link between dirt and guilt, and cleanliness and innocence, is built into our language. We talk about dirty jokes and laundering money. When we step to close too something morally unsavory ... we say, 'I wanted to take a shower'" (2007, 8–9). Perceptions of "dirty" and "clean" often function as binaries within ontologies that dichotomize nature and culture. Dirtiness is classified with base bodily functions and associated with nature, while cleanliness is aligned with pursuits of the mind, godliness, and culture. Cultural studies scholar Phyllis Palmer maintains that in the United States, "we tend to believe that attitudes toward dirt and hygiene result from the logical unfolding of precise scientific knowledge about cleanliness and health" (1989, 140). Scientific and medical knowledge of health and perceptions of hygiene have vacillated greatly throughout western history and have therefore affected cultural understandings of what humans perceive as "dirty" or "clean." Palmer notes that "historians are just beginning to study Americans' changing standards of dirt" (1989, 139), and what these views communicate about social, cultural, and material interactions. Scientifically, culturally, historically, and geographically, the words dirt and soil assume a multiplicity of meanings. While there are diverse understandings of soil and dirt throughout the world, my approaches are situated within the global north, specifically the United States and Europe, as that is where most case studies in this book occur (apart from *Las Mariposas* in Chapter 3).

The field of soil science is relatively new, gaining traction in the 20th century. In the global north, there are vast and multidisciplinary approaches to soil science. For instance, some technoscience approaches center on productionist logic, stressing crop yield. Other methods, like the foodweb model, focus on interconnected organismal webs within the soil, understanding soil as a multispecies living entity. Soil science, science, and ecology are not fixed or universal terms. Nor are understandings of soil and dirt. They shift and change in relation to time, space, geography, worldview, history, and politics. Throughout *Choreographing Dirt*, I use the word dirt to specifically denote soil that has been removed from its original ecological context and situated within the framework of performance, which transforms it into dirt.

Discourses of the Anthropocene

This book, and its exploration of dirt's biogeocultography in performance, is situated within the context of the current epoch and its contingent discourses and debates. The planet is undergoing rapid and considerable ecological change. Ecosystems are becoming more fragmented and extinction rates are extremely high (Roberson et al. 2020). There is enough trash in the Great Pacific Ocean Patch to completely cover all of France, Germany, and Spain (Lebreton et al. 2018). We are just beginning to see the impacts of climate change – glaciers are melting, coastlines are eroding, and incidences of extreme weather are increasing (Stott 2016). Moreover, there are myriad ecological dilemmas and disasters occurring on a regular basis, from nuclear waste, water contamination, and oil spills, to deforestation, over-fishing, ozone depletion, droughts, and fires. Movement is a latent aspect of these complex ecological issues. For instance, where does trash go? How do climate change and extreme weather force the movement of humans and more-than-humans? How does toxicity and contamination move matter and organisms?

Chemist Paul Crutzen and biologist Eugene Stoermer argue that humans have had such a profound impact on the earth in the past 600 years that evidence of human existence will forever be present in the earth's strata. They argue that the present should be dubbed the "Anthropocene," or the "Age of Humans," a new geological epoch defined by the ecological catastrophe of modern civilization. The Anthropocene is a contentious concept within many disciplines and worldviews. Scientists, scholars, philosophers, and many others debate whether we are indeed in a new epoch, and if so, when it began and what it should be called. What remains clear is that the earth is changing. What is less clear is when this change began and what caused it.

Crutzen and Stoermer originally marked the beginning of the Anthropocene at ~1800 C.E., heralding the Industrial Revolution and James Watt's improvements to the steam engine as significant forces in this epoch shift (2000). Geographers Simon L. Lewis and Mark A. Maslin, however, question whether the Industrial Revolution was indeed the beginning of the Anthropocene. Based on their analyses of stratigraphic data, they suggest the 1600s (possibly even earlier) as one possible origin of the Anthropocene, resulting from the effects of colonialism. They state, "The impacts of the meeting of Old and New World human populations, including the geologically unprecedented homogenization of Earth's biota – may serve to mark the beginning of the Anthropocene" (2015, 175). Presenting evidence for an alternate Anthropocene date is important because each potential date and timeline has different geopolitical and social implications. As Lewis and Maslin assert:

> defining an early start date may, in political terms, "normalize" global environmental change. Meanwhile, agreeing a later start date related to the Industrial Revolution may … be used to assign historical responsibility for carbon dioxide emissions to particular countries or regions during the industrial era. More broadly, the formal definition of the Anthropocene makes scientists arbiters, to an extent, of the human–environment relationship, itself an act with consequences beyond geology.
>
> (2015, 171)

In this regard, identifying the beginning of the Anthropocene is a scientific endeavor with profound implications for how humans understand global climate change, and who might be responsible for initiating and facilitating this change.

The Anthropocene is also contested within the social sciences and humanities. The fields of postcolonial studies, political science, feminist studies, and environmental humanities, to name a few, are all engaged in discussing the

Introduction 9

validity, definition, timing, and implications of the Anthropocene. Historian Dipesh Chakrabarty notes that one problem of the Anthropocene is the lack of nuance when discussing the "negative" impact of "humans" on the earth. For example, many scientists and authors assign blame for the Anthropocene and its concomitant issues to humanity as one homogeneous unit. Chakrabarty argues that this does not account for regionalism and variation in contributions among geographic places. He states, "the scientific literature on global warming thinks of humans as constitutively one – a species, a collectivity whose commitment to fossil-fuel based, energy-consuming civilization is now a threat to that civilization" (2001, 2). Social anthropologist Zoe Todd (Métis) also affirms the "hegemonic tendencies" of Anthropocene narratives, arguing that "the complex and paradoxical experiences of diverse people … including the ongoing damage of colonial and imperialist agendas, can be lost when the narrative is collapsed to a universalizing species paradigm" (2015, 252, 244). To disrupt generalizing accounts of the Anthropocene, Todd calls for an examination of where these "discourses are situated, who is defining the problems, and who decides the players involved" (2015, 252). Similarly, Chakrabarty endorses a more nuanced approach that does not group people and places together under one umbrella of "humanity" but instead focuses on "intrahuman justice," which examines and questions the advent of the Anthropocene and the "uneven impacts of climate change" (2011, 14).

Social scientist Macarena Gómez-Barris also contends that the broadness of the Anthropocene does not contextualize the "histories of racial thought and settler colonialism that are imposed upon categorizations of biodiversity" (2017, 4). She argues that the problem of the Anthropocene is actually very specific, that colonial capitalism has consumed the earth's resources, constructed racialized bodies, and systematically destroyed them "through dispossession, enslavement, and then producing the planet as a corporate bioterritory" (2017, 4). Scholar of inhuman geography, Kathryn Yusoff, maintains that the Anthropocene both reinforces and is a product of colonialism (2018, 62). She argues that the Anthropocene "neatly erases histories of racism that were incubated through the regulatory structure of geologic relations" (2018, 2). Because colonialism racialized bodies and transformed matter into extractive capital, Gómez-Barris and Yusoff both identify it as a critical force in the construction of the Anthropocene.

Discussing the environmental impacts of settler colonialism for many Indigenous peoples in North America, environmental justice scholar Kyle Powys Whyte (Citizen Potawatomi Nation) explains that many Indigenous people already consider themselves to be living in a dystopia. He clarifies that an Indigenous understanding of dystopia is different from a non-Indigenous understanding. Due to the consequences of settler colonialism many Indigenous peoples "are no longer able to relate locally to many of the plants and animals that are significant to them … [thus they] already inhabit what our ancestors would have likely characterized as a dystopian future" (2017, 207).

Living in a dystopia affects Indigenous approaches to conservation and restoration. As Whyte asserts,

> [Indigenous approaches] are not only about whether to conserve or let go of certain species. Rather, they are about what relationships between humans and certain plants and animals we should focus on in response to the challenges we face, given that we have already lost so many plants and animals that matter to our societies.
>
> (2017, 207)

The effects of settler colonialism are ongoing and continue to inflict violence and injustices on many Indigenous peoples by disrupting their relationships with animals, plants, matter, and humans.

Because of the complexities and reductivism of the Anthropocene as a nomenclature, other names have been introduced to address some of the issues raised by Chakrabarty, Todd, Gómez-Barris, and others. Sociologist Eileen Crist claims that the Anthropocene neutralizes the language surrounding ecological devastation. She asserts that,

> The Anthropocene discourse veers away from environmentalism's dark idiom of destruction, depredation, rape, loss, devastation, deterioration, and so forth of the natural world into the tame vocabulary that humans are changing, shaping, transforming, or altering the biosphere, and, in the process, creating novel ecosystems and anthropogenic biomes.
>
> (2016, 18)

The Capitalocene (Moore 2016) is an alternate classification that has gained traction. Sociologist Jason Moore describes the Capitalocene as "an ugly word for an ugly system," stating that "the Capitalocene signifies capitalism as a way of organizing nature – as a multispecies, situated, capitalist world ecology" (2016, 6). This term more explicitly captures the role of capitalism in turning nature into a resource for human consumption. Other terms such as the Chthulucene (Haraway 2016), Technocene (Hornborg 2015), Manthropocene (Raworth 2014), and Plantocene (Haenggi and Kennedy 2020) have also been proffered. While these classifications might better linguistically account for the complexity and nuance of our current epoch, for better or worse, it seems that the Anthropocene has entered the cultural lexicon.

The situated destructive practices and ideologies that created, and persist within the current epoch, are unwieldy, complicated, and multi-scalar. They are perhaps best understood as "wicked problems," which public health scientist Atul Gawande describes as, "messy, ill-defined, more complex than we fully grasp, and open to multiple interpretations based on one's point of view" (2012). Perhaps at first glance performance may not seem like a productive space for addressing the "wicked problems" of the current epoch. Or maybe it seems naively hopeful to think that performance has the potential to affect any meaningful kind of change. I would argue, however, that the underlying situated causes of the current ecological crises are fundamentally anthropogenic and, thus, cultural. The responsibility of contending with "wicked" ecological problems often falls on STEM disciplines; but addressing the complexities of these issues and working toward change require perspectives from multiple disciplines, including performance, theatre, and dance. Using the framework of choreography to think through the "wicked problem" of the bags of Fukushima dirt illuminates how the dirt's movement is a force that structures other movements and alters biological and cultural understandings of soil. Theatre scholar Wendy Arons stresses that "The need for theatre scholars to investigate the ways in which theater and performance have shaped and/or might reshape our orientation to the natural world has not become any less urgent as the threat of global warming (and its attendant ecological and social catastrophes) looms ever nearer" (2010, 149). Foster further suggests that scholars and practitioners have the responsibility to treat bodies as agents of change because choreographic processes enable "bodies [to] create new images, relationships, concepts, and reflections" (1995, 3). She also maintains that scholars should approach "the body's involvement in any activity with an assumption of potential agency to participate in or resist whatever forms of cultural production are underway" (Foster 1995, 3).

While performance and dance studies may enable scholars to use disciplinary approaches like embodiment and movement to think through the Anthropocene's "wicked problems," others argue that such approaches are too optimistic or naïve. For instance, Lavery contends that theatre and performance tend to make "largely positive – perhaps even hyperbolic – claims for theatre's capacity to bring about behaviour change, more often than not through some ecstatic or enchanted immersion in 'environment'" (2016, 229). Of course, theatre and performance have varied limitations and quantifying the ability of the arts to change behaviors and mindsets is difficult, if not impossible. Performance scholar Lisa Woynarski argues that while performance may not be "a blunt instrument for social change," it can function as a space to "help us understand our failure better" (2020, 220). Similarly, theatre scholar Theresa J. May acknowledges that while theatre in the United States has contributed to settler ideologies and environmental injustices, she still maintains that it contains the potential to "contribute to civic and ecological justice and healing" (2021, 7). I tend to concur with Woynarski and May that while performance, particularly in the United States, has contributed to social and environmental injustices, it can also serve as a productive space to think through failure. Additionally, if many of our epoch's "wicked problems" concern the displacement of humans and more-than-humans (e.g., radioactive dirt, trash, climate change, and extreme weather), how might choreography, and to a greater extent dance and performance studies, offer perspectives and practices to address these complex issues? As I demonstrate by analyzing

12 *Introduction*

the intersections of ecology and environmental racism (*The America Play*), extractive capitalism (*The Rite of Spring*), interactions of human and more-than-human bodies (*Las Mariposas*), and an eco-ethics of care (*Messengers Divinos*), I think that dance and performance studies can offer spaces to grapple with the hope and despair of the current epoch and address the multifaceted dilemmas of the Anthropocene.

Methods: Materiality, Choreography, and Performance

Choreographing Dirt places dance studies, theatre and performance studies, the environmental humanities, science, and posthumanism in dialogue together, to explore the intersections of ecology, theatre/performance, and dance/movement. The three primary frameworks I use in the book are materiality, choreography, and performance. The following section delineates theories within these frameworks that inform my approaches.

While a "material turn" may be a recent development in western epistemologies, it is by no means "new." Discussing the "material turn" in western scholarship, Todd points out that western scholars working in posthumanism and new materialisms often replicate Indigenous thought without acknowledging Indigenous knowledges or scholars. By not citing and recognizing the labor of Indigenous scholars, Todd argues that,

> the Ontological Turn – with its breathless "realisations" that animals, the climate, water, "atmospheres" and non-human presences like ancestors and spirits are sentient and possess agency, that "nature" and "culture", "human" and "animal" may not be so separate after all – is itself perpetuating the exploitation of Indigenous peoples.
>
> (2016, 13)

As cultural geographer Juanita Sundberg asserts, "posthumanist theorists often make the mistake of assuming the nature/culture binary is universal and not localized within Western/Anglo-European thought" (2014, 33). She challenges scholars to "seek out scholarship rooted in non-dualistic epistemic traditions" (2014, 35). Todd affirms that by not including Indigenous scholars in discussions of the more-than-human, "we perpetuate the white supremacy of the academy" (2016, 18). Prompted by Todd and Sundberg's calls, I strive to situate knowledges and consult Indigenous scholars alongside non-Indigenous scholars. I am not positing that the significance of matter is "new." Rather, I contend that analyzing the material aspects of performance, situated and created within anthropocentric ontologies, reveals the limits of western dualisms. Particularly in Chapters 2 and 4, I draw from scholars who theorize ontology from Indigenous cosmologies, such as Zoe Todd, Vanessa Watts, Te Kawehau Hoskins, Dwayne Trevor Donald, and Michelle Murphey, as well as those working within western frameworks (the same frameworks in which most of the performances were created).

Following Todd and Sundberg and recognizing the history of white supremacy in western academic traditions, I feel it is important to situate myself and my own knowledge to make visible these contexts and histories which are often obscured. I am a white ciswoman of settler ancestry who currently resides and works on the territories of multiple Indigenous nations who were dispossessed and removed, specifically the Tonkawa, Tawakoni, Hueco, Sana, Wichita, and Coahuiltecan peoples. As indicated in the earlier description of my botanical excursions, my understandings of nature and ecology were developed within a western framework. Coming to terms with my own anthropocentrism through these embodied experiences enabled me to contend with the limits of western dualisms more thoroughly. I exercise reflexivity throughout the book in the ways that I grapple with western ideologies and ontologies, in which I am also implicated.

While my approaches to materiality are shaped by situated knowledges and reflexivity, my approaches to choreography are grounded in understanding it as the sequencing of human and more-than-human movement. Foster's theorization of choreography as a "structuring of movement, not necessarily the movement of human beings," is crucial to my analyses (1995, 2); as is environmental humanities scholar Carrie Rohman's understanding of it as "the intricate ways in which life and species forces *move* and shape themselves in ever-surprising combinations and patterns that momentarily cohere only to become something else in the next instant" (2018, 13, italics in original). For both Foster and Rohman, choreography is not limited to the human realm, it also includes more-than-human beings. Similarly, performance studies scholar Julia Handschuh questions how an attunement to the more-than-human world could change movement patterns:

> How are our understandings of power and subjectivities changed if, instead of being defined by a single call-and-response of one human to another, we instead turn toward the soil, a river, or a storm? Understanding our identities as constituted by both human and environmental relations thus requires that we give credence to the landscapes we inhabit.
> (2014, 160)

The choreography of ecological matter matters for multiple reasons; it matters on its own terms, it matters because it affects the movements of other things, and it matters because it can expose the extractive logics of capitalism that reduce matter to a resource (and contribute to climate change). Thus, analyzing the movement of ecological matter through a choreographic framework also reveals the ways in which displacement destroys lives and habitats and makes connections between the extraction of matter and environmental and social injustices. For performance and dance scholars Ric Allsopp and

André Lepecki, the politics of movement relate to materiality, as the questions governing geopolitical and bio-political mobility are "essentially choreographic ones" (2010, 1). That is, who or what can move freely or who or what is forcibly displaced is dependent on geo/bio-political contexts which can expose underlying injustices. As geographical, biological, and ecological issues come to matter in movement, ecocriticism is well suited to explore them.

This book also builds on the ecocritical work of performance scholars May, Arons, Woynarski, Una Chaudhuri, and others, whose scholarship critically examines the intersections of ecology and performance. For May, ecocriticism is "a critical (discursive) perspective on cultural performance (from theatre, film, and literature to zoos, amusement parks, and social protests) afforded and informed by the science of ecology and the greening fire it has precipitated across disciplines" (2007, 95, 97). Specifically applying an ecocritical approach to performance, May and Arons present ecodramaturgy as a method that shifts the focus of performance analysis and practice beyond the human by acknowledging that humans are comprised of and in constant entanglement with other matter, species, and ecological systems (2012, 6).[10] Building on their work, Woynarski develops ecodramaturgies, which she posits as

> a way of understanding how... performance practices make ecological meaning and interact with the material more-than-human world ... Thinking ecologically requires a shift in perspective to decenter the human, question neoliberal environmental logic and reimagine the nature/culture binary.
>
> (2020, 10)

Ecodramaturgies applied to performance practices and analyses can foreground the more-than-human world and expose environmental and human injustices.

While ecological approaches to dance and performance continue to develop in exciting and significant ways, there is still much work required to shift western/Anglo-European assumptions that the "subject is always already human," which posthumanist scholar Cary Wolfe attributes to an "institution of speciesism" (2003, 1). Anthropocentrism still dominates the arts and humanities (and I would argue, STEM fields as well) as Chaudhuri asserts, "the arts have not, so far, managed to disrupt ... the persistence of a fundamentally anthropocentric, non-ecological perspective on life... enough to make a difference" (Preece and Allen 2015, 105). The earth is home to approximately 5 million different species, and human bodies contain more bacterial cells than human cells (Costello et al. 2013, 413). In this way, a performer on a stage – human or more-than-human – is hardly an individual, but rather a complex assemblage of millions of organisms. Thus, every interaction among humans and more-than-human beings is an ecologically charged event. How then, might we approach these relationships in performance? How do we acknowledge and ethically engage with more-than-human matter on stage? *Choreographing Dirt* explores these questions by using an ecocritical perspective to examine the biogeocultography of dirt in performance and its capacity to challenge anthropocentrism and expose environmental injustice.

Choreographing Dirt: Chapter Structure

Displacing dirt for performance purposes is by no means a new practice. For instance, in 1983, artist Allan Kaprow began a series of performative "dirt exchanges" that would eventually become renowned in performance spheres as "Trading Dirt." In these transactions, Kaprow dug up dirt, placed it in the back of his pickup truck, and drove it to different geographical locations to swap it with other people. In one exchange, Kaprow recounts taking a "bucket of good garden dirt" from his personal garden and exchanging it for some "heavy-duty Buddhist dirt" from underneath a Buddhist Zen Center (Kaprow 2004, 163). To transfer the dirt, Kaprow crawled underneath the Zen Center, beneath the place where his teacher meditated, dug up some of the "Buddhist dirt," and emptied his "good garden dirt" into the space. Eventually he exchanged the "Buddhist dirt" with a woman who operated a local farm, asking her if they could "trade dirt?" He collected the "farm dirt" and emptied the "Buddhist dirt" into the freshly dug hole. This process of trading dirt went on for about three years with, "no real beginning or end. The stories began to add up to a very long story, and with each retelling they changed," recalls Kaprow (2004, 163). "When I stopped being interested in the process … I put the last bucket of dirt back into the garden" (Kaprow 2004, 163).

From a contemporary perspective, Kaprow's dirt exchanges might seem disconcerting, as they appear to disregard the possible ecological impacts of "trading dirt," like the spread of invasive species, parasitic or toxic fungi, disturbance of soil fauna, and the potential spread of contaminants or chemicals. Considering current large-scale invasive species problems in the United States, the idea of exchanging dirt is perhaps questionable at best. It strikes me, however, that these exchanges still serve as fecund sites where the boundaries among performance, movement, and ecology are blurred. They are sites where ecological thinking becomes imperative. Ecological thinking, according to philosopher Timothy Morton, is not just about human and more-than-human relationships; "it has to do with love, loss, despair, and compassion. It has to do with depression and psychosis. It has to do with capitalism…it has to do with… open-mindedness, and wonder. It has to do with doubt, confusion, and skepticism…it has to do with coexistence" (Morton 2010, 2). Soil, dirt, and their extended ecosystems are part of these ecological and discursive entanglements and analyzing them within the framework of performance exposes complex webs of coexistence.

16 *Introduction*

"Trading Dirt," much like the bags of Fukushima dirt, illustrates the intersections of ecology, performance, and movement that perambulate through this book. The choreography of soil is significant. In the case of "Trading Dirt," the movement appears to be without thought of the potential ecological consequences. Exhibiting that humans can view soil (and by extension other ecological matter) as something that can be displaced and utilized for their own purposes. The ecological ramifications of these movements emphasize the porosity among ecological matter and other bodies. It is these permeable sites, where the boundaries of performance, history, and ecology blur.

The texts and performances in the following chapters are connected through movement and materiality. Each chapter explores the choreography of dirt through what I designate as *performative taphonomy* (that the presence of exhumed ecological matter on stage and page – e.g., dirt – "does" something)[11] and *biogeocultography* (the movement of ecological matter creates biological, geographic, and cultural meaning). To acknowledge the inherent anthropocentricism of speaking on behalf of dirt, I strategically activate an "ecological anthropomorphism," "[an] anthropomorphism that disrupts the anthropocentric hierarchy through recognition of the capacity for agency and action in the more-than-human and questions binary-making practices" (Woynarski 2015, 24). Through my analysis of dirt as a performer, I employ an "ecological anthropomorphism," which decenters the human and gestures toward a non-anthropocentric approach to performance. The performance and the critical analysis of the performance are enhanced through an acknowledgment of dirt as a vital performer. Even though the prominence of dirt varies in each performance, its inclusion "does" something. By disinterring particulates of the past (contained in the dirt) and placing them on stage, the dirt performs for human spectators and performs in its own interests.

Chapter 1, Performative Taphonomy: Excavating and Exhuming the Past in Suzan-Lori Parks's *The America Play*, concentrates on soil in Parks's *The America Play* (1994). Over the course of the play, the Foundling Father – a Black gravedigger who dresses like Abraham Lincoln – digs over 723 holes. I analyze the Foundling Father's relationship with the soil and argue that it has somatic, ecological, and historical significance. While many Parks scholars draw attention to the *archaeological* discourses the playwright activates through the digging metaphor, I examine the taphonomical[12] and historiographical implications revealed in the gravedigger's interaction with the literal dirt itself. The physical labor and repetition of the Foundling Father's digging convey meaning regarding the history and class structure of enslaved people in the United States, many of whose experiences have been omitted from historical narratives because of white supremacy. Using Gilles Deleuze and Félix Guattari's theories of affect and immanent philosophy, I argue that the Foundling Father *becomes* Lincoln in the affective sense; he unearths concepts on the plane of immanence that reimagine or "reterritorialize" history. Ultimately, this affective relationship, layered on an invocation of enslavement, and predicated on a literal descent into historical earth, allows for a powerful interrogation and reconstruction of historical narratives in the United States. This accomplishes what I term a "performative taphonomy," as both historiography and taphonomy seek to understand material remains and the (ecological) processes that preserved their existence through time.

Chapter 2, Staging Extraction: Peat's Vitality in Pina Bausch's *The Rite of Spring*, focuses on the materiality of the peat moss used in Bausch's adaptation of *The Rite of Spring* (1975). In her production, a thick layer of peat coats the stage and as the dancers move, the peat flies into the air and coats their bodies. This chapter explores the biological composition, environmental significance, and historical implications of peat to demonstrate that its use in *The Rite of Spring* conveys distinct meanings that are situated in its geographical and cultural contexts. Peat bogs have preserved human remains for thousands of years, and researchers believe some of these remains to be the result of ancient rites and rituals. Using the theory of Vanessa Watts, Stacy Alaimo, and Chaudhuri, I examine the peat's vitality, discuss the significance of the dancers performing this piece in a substance that potentially contains human remains, and consider the ethical dimensions of displacing the peat. I argue that the peat's presence in *The Rite of Spring* stages a rupture that exposes the extractive logics of capitalism that contribute to climate change and erase history.

Chapter 3, A Dirty *Pas De Deux*: Dirt, Skin, and "Trans-corporeality" in Eveoke Dance Theatre's *Las Mariposas*, delves deeper into dirt by examining the microscopic organisms that reside within it and on human skin in the dance-theatre production of *Las Mariposas* (2010). *Las Mariposas*, an imaginative adaptation of Julia Alvarez's novel *In the Time of the Butterflies* (1994), tells the story of the Mirabal sisters, who led an underground resistance in the 1950s against Dominican dictator Rafael Trujillo. In this production, large bins of dirt are used to perform an interpretation of the murder of the Mirabal sisters. The choreography of this killing yields a violent and grotesquely beautiful performance of stylized frenetic movement all while dirt is spewed into the air, colliding with the bodies of the dancers. Pairing dancer interviews with Gilles Deleuze and Félix Guattari's theories of affect, I explore the ways in which the physical interactions among the dancers and dirt enabled them to form affective relationships that restructured their material composition. Using the theory of Rosi Braidotti, Stacy Alaimo, Diana Taylor, and Woynarski, I argue that these affective relationships disrupt anthropocentric conceptions of humanity by revealing the presence of other invisible materials (protozoa, bacteria, etc.). This close reading of *Las Mariposas* maintains that humans – in performance and everyday life – are not discretely bounded, but rather their corporeal boundaries are permeable and dynamic. The dancer and dirt relationships in *Las Mariposas* disrupt anthropocentrism and demonstrate that the performer is not always human.

18 *Introduction*

Chapter 4, Mycelium in Motion: Choreographing Care in Iván-Daniel Espinosa's *Messengers Divinos*, explores the partnering of humans and mycelium (networks of fungi) in the durational Butoh performance *Messengers Divinos: A Meditation on Time, Space, Corporeality, & Consciousness* (2018). Incorporating the science of mycology into his creative process, Espinosa's choreography engages the heterogeneous temporalties of fungi and utilizes techniques that center relationality. Here, I focus on *Messengers Divinos* as well as Espinosa's choreographic process, analyzing them through María Puig de la Bellacasa's "speculative ethics of care," and Dwayne Trevor Donald's "Indigenous Métissage." I argue that *Messengers Divinos* demonstrates a performance praxis that grapples with on an ecological ethics of care.

Each chapter closely examines 20th- and 21st-century text and performances that occur within North America, Central America, and Europe. Through my analyses, I demonstrate how the incorporation of something so seemingly humble as dirt can reveal micro-level interactions between species – e.g., the interplay between microscopic skin bacteria and soil protozoa – and macro-level interactions – e.g., the transformation of peat to a greenhouse gas. *Choreographing Dirt* examines nothing more, and nothing less, than literal dirt in performance. It demonstrates that the choreography of dirt evokes an intricate reconsideration of ecology and performance in the Anthropocene.

Notes

1 These descriptions are from images of the Fukushima countryside and a temporary storage site in Tomioka, Fukushima Prefecture published in Nippon.com (2019) and *The Mainichi* (2015).
2 The most powerful earthquake in Japan to date.
3 The half-lives of these materials differ greatly, ranging from several days to over 30 years (Hashimoto et al. 2022).
4 In *The Spell of the Sensuous: Perception and Language in a More-Than-Human World*, David Abram uses "more-than-human" to describe the larger community that includes, "along with the humans, the multiple nonhuman entities that constitute the local landscape, from the diverse plants and myriad animals – birds, mammals, fish, reptiles, insects – that inhabit or migrate through the region, to the particular winds and weather patterns that inform the local geography, as well as the various landforms – forests, rivers, caves, mountains – that lend their specific character to the surrounding earth." David Abram, *The Spell of the Sensuous: Perception and Language in a More-Than-Human World* (New York: Pantheon Books, 1996), 6–7.
5 I use ecology here, and throughout the book, in its scientific context to reference the relationships among living things and their environments. That is, the complex multispecies webs in which humans and more-than-humans are enmeshed.
6 I use performance here to mean the way that nature (or matter) through its vitality performs for its own reasons. Prudence Gibson and Catriona Sandilands apply this to plants, stating that plants perform "in their own interests [and] as part of a multispecies network of performativity in which . . showiness, smelliness, and eventfulness combine in specific ways to bring about desired ends such as pollination" (2021, 2).

7 I place nature in quotes here to acknowledge its construction as a term that is not fixed or stable. It carries different meanings within different historical and social moments, and across and within cultures. In western binary frameworks, it is often considered to be in opposition to "culture." While this understanding of nature holds true throughout the book, I only use the quotes here in my first use of the word.

8 I trained in tap, jazz, and ballet and minored in dance in college. I worked in arts administration at a professional ballet company before returning to graduate school. I still enjoy teaching and creating devised movement and choreography.

9 I use dirt, here, in an expanded sense to include all the "out of place" matter I discuss in this book (e.g., peat and fungi). As I argue in different ways throughout the book, removing matter and placing it on stage makes it "out of place," to different degrees, capacities, and scales.

10 The term ecodramaturgy was originally coined by Theresa J. May in 2010 (Arons and May 2012, 4).

11 Performative taphonomy is discussed more comprehensively in Chapter 1.

12 The study of the processes of burial, decay, and fossilization.

References

Alaimo, Stacy. 2008. "Trans-Corporeal Feminisms and the Ethical Space of Nature." In *Material Feminisms*, edited by Stacy Alaimo and Susan Hekman, 237–264. Bloomington: Indiana University Press.

Arons, Wendy. 2010. "Beyond the Nature/Culture Divide: Challenges from Ecocriticism and Evolutionary Biology for Theater Historiography." In *Theater Historiography: Critical Interventions*, edited by Henry Bial and Scott Magelssen, 148–161. Ann Arbor: The University of Michigan Press.

Arons, Wendy, and Theresa J. May. 2012. "Introduction." In *Readings in Performance and Ecology*, edited by Wendy Arons and Theresa J. May, 3–12. New York: Palgrave.

Ashenburg, Katherine. 2007. *The Dirt on Clean: An Unsanitized History*. New York: North Point Press.

Bardgett, Richard D. 2005. *The Biology of Soil: A Community and Ecosystem Approach (Biology of Habitats)*. New York: Oxford University Press, Inc.

Birge, Hannah E., Richard T. Conant, Ronald F. Follett, Michelle L. Haddix, Sherri J. Morris, Sieglinde S. Snapp, Matthew D. Wallenstein, and Eldor A. Paul. 2015. "Soil respiration Is Not Limited by Reductions in Microbial Biomass during Long-Term Soil Incubations." *Soil Biology and Biochemistry* 81: 304–310.

Chakrabarty, Dipesh. 2011. "The Climate of History: Four Thesis." *Postcolonial Studies* 14, no. 3: 197–222.

Costello, Mark J., Robert M. May, and Nigel E. Stork. 2013. "Can We Name Earth's Species Before They Go Extinct?" *Science* 339, no. 6118: 413–416.

Crist, Eileen. 2016. "On the Poverty of Nomenclature." In *Anthropocene Or Capitalocene? Nature, History, and the Crisis of Capitalism*, edited by Jason W. Moore, 129–147. Binghamton: PM Press.

Crutzen, Paul J., and Eugene F. Stoermer. 2000. "The "Anthropocene." *Global Change Newsletter* 41: 17.

Douglas, Mary. 1966. *Purity and Danger: An Analysis of the Concepts of Pollution and Taboo*. London: Ark Paperbacks.

Foster, Susan Leigh. 1995. "An Introduction to Moving Bodies." In *Choreographing History*, edited by Susan Leigh Foster, 3–24. Bloomington: Indiana University Press.

Gawande, Atul. 2012. "Something Wicked this Way Comes." *The New Yorker*. June 28, 2012.
Gibson, Prudence, and Catriona Sandilands. 2021. "Introduction: Plant Performance." *Performance Philosophy* 6, no. 2: 1–23.
Gómez-Barris, Macarena. 2017. *The Extractive Zone: Social Ecologies and Decolonial Perspectives*. Durham: Duke University Press.
Haraway, Donna J. 2016. *Staying with the Trouble: Making kin in the Chthulucene*. Durham: Duke University Press.
Hashimoto, Shoji, Masabumi Komatsu, and Satoru Miura. 2022. "Radioactive Materials Released by the Fukushima Nuclear Accident." In *Forest Radioecology in Fukushima*, 1–10. Singapore: Springer.
Haenggi, Andrea and Christopher Kennedy. 2020. "The Emergent Plantocene Weedy Vegetal Agency, Radical Embodiment, and Ruderalism X Action(ism)." *Medium*. October 19, 2020.
Hornborg, Alf. 2015. "The Political Ecology of the Technocene: Uncovering Ecologically Unequal Exchange in the World-System." In *The Anthropocene and the Global Environmental Crisis*, 57–69. London: Routledge.
Kaprow, Allan. 2004. "Just Doing." In *The Performance Studies Reader*, edited by Henry Bial, 159–163. New York: Routledge.
Kristeva, Julia. 1982. *Powers of Horror*. Translated by Louis-Ferdinand Celine. New York: Columbia University Press.
Lavery, Carl. 2019. "Introduction." In *Performance and Ecology: What Can Theatre Do?* edited by Carl Lavery, 1–8. Oxon: Routledge.
Lebreton, L., B. Slat, F. Ferrari, et al. 2018. "Evidence that the Great Pacific Garbage Patch Is. Rapidly Accumulating Plastic." *Scientific Reports* 8: 4666.
Lewis, Simon L., and Mark A Maslin. 2015. "Defining the Anthropocene." *Nature* 519, no. 7542: 171–180.
Logan, William Bryant. 2007. *Dirt the Ecstatic Skin of the Earth*. London: W. W. Norton.
May, Theresa J. 2007. "Beyond Bambi: Toward a Dangerous Ecocriticism in Theatre Studies." *Theatre Topics* 17, no. 2: 95–110.
May, Theresa J. 2021. *Earth Matters on Stage*. London: Routledge.
McCurry, Justin. 2019. "Fukushima Grapples with Toxic Soil That No One wants." *The Guardian*. March 11, 2019. Accessed August 6, 2022. https://www.theguardian.com/world/2019/mar/11/fukushima-toxic-soil-disaster-radioactive.
Ministry of the Environment, Japan. 2015. "FY2014 Decontamination Report." March 2015. Accessed August 6, 2022. http://josen.env.go.jp/en/policy_document/pdf/decontamination_report1503_full.pdf.
Ministry of the Environment, Japan. 2018. "Environmental Remediation in Japan." March 2018. Accessed August 6, 2022. http://josen.env.go.jp/en/pdf/progressseet_progress_on_cleanup_efforts.pdf.
Moore, Jason W. 2016. "Introduction." In *Anthropocene Or Capitalocene? Nature, History, and the Crisis of Capitalism*, edited by Jason W. Moore. Binghamton: PM Press.
Morton, Timothy. 2010. *The Ecological Thought*. Cambridge: Harvard University Press.
Nardi, James B. 2007. *Life in the Soil: A Guide for Naturalists and Gardeners*. Chicago: University of Chicago Press.

Nippon.com. 2019. Fukushima Eight Years Later: Black Sacks and Lonely Children. April 5, 2019. Accessed August 6, 2022.

Ohnuma, Tohru, and Keizo Ishii. 2019. "Study of Soil Particles Contaminated with Radioactive Cesium in Pond Sediment." *Cogent Engineering* 6, no. 1: 1–12.

Oxford English Dictionary. 2013a. "Dirt." Web. April 11, 2013. Accessed April 11, 2013. http://www.oed.com.maurice.bgsu.edu.

Oxford English Dictionary. 2013b. "Soil." April 11, 2013. Accessed April 11, 2013. http://www.oed.com.maurice.bgsu.edu.

Palmer, Phyllis M. 1989. *Domesticity and Dirt: Housewives and Domestic Servants in the United States, 1920-1945*. Philadelphia: Temple University Press.

Preece, Bronwyn, and Jess Allen. 2015. "A 'Turn to the Species:' Una Chaudhuri Reflects on some of the Ethical Challenges and Possibilities that are Emerging from a Decade of Ecological Performance Practice and Scholarship." *Performing Ethos: International Journal of Ethics in Theatre & Performance* 4, no. 2: 103–111.

Raloff, Janet 2008. "Dirt is Not Soil." *Science News*.

Raworth, Kate. 2014. "Must the Anthropocene be a Manthropocene." *The Guardian*. October 20, 2014.

Roberson, Emily Brin, Anne Frances, Kayri Havens, Joyce Maschinski, Abby Meyer, and Lisa Ott. 2020. "Fund Plant Conservation to Solve Biodiversity crisis." *Science* 367, no. 6475: 258.

Solnit, Rebecca. 2001. *As Eve Said to the Serpent: On Landscape, Gender, and Art*. Athens: University of Georgia Press.

Stott, Peter. 2016. "How Climate Change Affects Extreme Weather Events." *Science* 352, no. 6293: 1517–1518.

Sundberg, Juanita. 2014. "Decolonizing Posthumanist Geographies." *Cultural Geographies* 21, no. 1: 33–47.

The Asahi Shimbun. 2022. "Radioactive Waste Stuck at 830 Sites with Nowhere to Go." March 3, 2022. Accessed August 6, 2022. https://www.asahi.com/ajw/articles/14562951.

The Mainichi. 2015. "Over 9 Million Bags of Nuclear Cleanup Waste Piled Up Across Fukushima Pref." December 10, 2015. Accessed August 6, 2022. https://mainichi.jp/english/articles/20151210/p2a/00m/0na/020000c.

Todd, Zoe. 2015. "Indigenizing the Anthropocene." *Art in the Anthropocene: Encounters among Aesthetics, Politics, Environments and Epistemologies* 241: 241–254.

Todd, Zoe. 2016. "An Indigenous Feminist's Take on the Ontological Turn: 'Ontology' Is Just Another Word for Colonialism." *Journal of Historical Sociology* 29, no. 1: 4–22.

Whyte, Kyle Powys. 2017. "Our Ancestors' Dystopia now: Indigenous Conservation and the Anthropocene." In *The Routledge Companion to the Environmental Humanities*, 222–231. London: Routledge.

Wolfe, Cary. 2003. *Animal Rites: American Culture, the Discourse of Species, and Posthumanist Theory*. Chicago: The University of Chicago Press.

Woynarski, Lisa. 2015. "A House of Weather and a Polar Bear Costume: Ecological Anthropomorphism in the Work of Fevered Sleep." *Performance Research* 20, no. 2: 24–32.

Woynarski, Lisa. 2020. *Ecodramaturgies: Theatre, Performance and Climate Change.* Switzerland: Palgrave Macmillan.

Yasunari, Teppei J., Andreas Stohl, Ryugo S. Hayano, John F. Burkhart, Sabine Eckhardt, and Tetsuzo Yasunari. 2011. "Cesium-137 Deposition and Contamination of Japanese Soils Due to the Fukushima Nuclear Accident." *Proceedings of the National Academy of Sciences* 108, no. 49: 19530–19534.

Yusoff, Kathryn. 2018. *A Billion Black Anthropocenes or None.* Minneapolis: University of Minnesota Press.

1 Performative Taphonomy

Excavating and Exhuming the Past in Suzan-Lori Parks's *The America Play*

While conducting a survey and excavation of the Ted Weiss Federal Building in Lower Manhattan in 1991, the General Services Administration (GSA) uncovered several intact human skeletons. The site had served as an African burial ground in the 17th and 18th centuries, and over the course of the next year, archaeologists unearthed 419 sets of human remains ("History and Culture" 2021).[1] Controversy developed over how the exhumed bodies were treated, and many communities protested the government's approach to the situation. Cultural geographer, Katherine McKittrick explains:

> the handling and remembering of the dead bodies [had] unraveled into a series of contestations... the black community staked a claim to the corpses and the burial ground to extend the political awareness of slavery, immense pressure was put on the scientific community to preserve the remains and gather data within a limited time frame ... [and] Few black scholars were invited to contribute to the excavation and analysis initially.
> (2013, 2)

Eventually, anthropologist Michael Blakey became the principal investigator. He and other Howard University anthropologists exhumed the remains and determined them to be predominantly enslaved Africans who lived in colonial New York (Chang 2020). In 2003, the GSA reinterred the bodies and Rodney Leon and AARIS architects built an outdoor memorial to commemorate the space. In 2006, President George W. Bush designated the site a national monument. For McKittrick, the African Burial Ground "opens up a spatial continuity between the living and the dead, between science and storytelling, and between past and present" (2013, 2). These material and metaphysical connections are a reminder that the past is never past; it is always informing the present. Blakey elucidates the significance of these relationships:

> Memorials are part of what it means to be human. And during slavery, the burial of the dead was very important – keenly important for Africans and African Americans whose humanity... was contested... and the African

DOI: 10.4324/9781003164234-2

Burial Ground is a memorial that celebrates not just death but the sanctity of Black life and the importance of our history.

(cited in Chang 2020)

The unearthing of these bodies revealed information that altered the historical, social, and biological context of the geographical area. It contributed to a deeper comprehension of the connections between the land and the people who lived, worked, and died there. The unearthing of the Black bodies housed in the soil reorients the historical narrative of the geographical site. The enslaved people who built what is now New York City are still present in the soil. Their bodies are "still interred, still biologically decaying and brushing up against the concrete" (McKittrick 2013, 2). These bodies alter the geography of Lower Manhattan and remake the history of the United States.

The African Burial Ground demonstrates how soil literally contains information that changes and influences the ways in which we understand and interpret the past. In the sciences, the study of what is present (or absent) in the soil after the death of an organism – that is, the processes of decomposition through time and fossilization – is called taphonomy. Geologist Ronald E. Martin explains that taphonomy comes "from the Greek *taphos* + *nomos*," meaning "the science of 'laws of burial'" (1999, 1, italics in original). Traces of the past are preserved within or erased from the soil, maintaining or deleting a record that informs our understanding of history. Taphonomical processes therefore parallel historical processes – at least according to postmodern theorist Linda Hutcheon, who posits that history is a discourse, a way in which we organize knowledge to make sense of the past. As she writes, "the meaning and shape are not *in the events*, but *in the systems* which make those past 'events' into present historical 'facts'" (1988, 89, italics in original). For both taphonomy and historiography, the meaning of the past is not in the materials that remain (in the soil) but in the conditions that enabled or hindered the presence of those (ecological) materials through time. Thus, taphonomical and historiographical pursuits seek to understand material remains and the processes that permitted or impeded their existence.

In this chapter I focus on soil in Suzan-Lori Parks's *The America Play* (1994), arguing that the Foundling Father's embodiment of Lincoln and his descent into the soil enact a biogeocultography, as he exhumes remains that alter the present and future. The physical labor of the Foundling Father's repetitive digging conveys meaning regarding the experiences of enslaved people and histories of environmental racism in the antebellum United States. Gilles Deleuze and Félix Guattari's affect theories are applied to demonstrate that the Foundling Father *becomes* Abraham Lincoln in the affective sense as he unearths concepts on the plane of immanence that reimagine or "reterritorialize" history. This affective relationship, layered with the experiences of enslaved people and predicated on a literal descent into the earth's strata, accomplishes a historiographical and performative taphonomy that unsettles the white geology of the Anthropocene.

Theatre and performance studies have much to gain by placing taphonomy in conversation with historiography, and the work of Suzan-Lori Parks provides a case in point. The African Burial Ground exhibits how an exhumation of soil reveals ecological and historical information that alters how we understand the past. Parks poetically invokes disinterment as a performative and historiographical act in much of her work. "[S]o much of African American history has been unrecorded, dismembered, washed out," she writes in her essay "Possession" (1995b, 4). "[O]ne of my tasks as playwright," she continues, "is to – through literature and the special strange relationship between theatre and real-life – locate the ancestral burial ground, dig for bones, find bones, hear the bones sing, write it down" (1995b, 4). Performance scholar, Sara L. Warner, designates Parks's preoccupation with exhumation as a "drama of disinterment," which is "[c]haracterized by a digging motif and the dis(re)memberment of corpses" (2008, 182). Warner argues that this "method of historicizing" (2008, 182) appears in Parks's *Venus* (1996), *The Death of the Last Black Man in the Whole Entire World* (1990), and *The America Play* (1994). But if digging through soil appears as a literary motif in much of Parks's work, I would add that it often functions quite literally – particularly in her first play, *The Sinners' Place* (1984); in *The America Play* (1994); and in her novel, *Getting Mother's Body* (2003). In fact, *The Sinners' Place* was rejected for production by the Mount Holyoke Theatre department because they told her, "You can't put dirt onstage! That's not a play!" (Garrett 2000, 22). Despite this initial rejection, Parks continued to be theatrically inclined toward "a lot of dirt onstage which was being dug at" (Garrett 2000, 22).

In Parks's work, dirt functions as an archaeological site where the "unrecorded" past can be exhumed. Her disinterment of the past queries what material remains (or absence) reveal about the assemblage of history. She not only exhumes the past but also takes the process one step further to "'make' history," by creating events that have "not yet been divined" (Parks 1995b, 4–5). In her reimagining of historical "events," Parks emphasizes how the past affects the present and the present affects the past, demonstrating that questioning "the history of History" is a vital task (Parks 1995b, 4–5). "The bones tell us what was, is, will be," she writes, "I'm working theatre like an incubator to create 'new' historical events" (1995b, 4–5). Theatre scholar Haike Frank argues, "[b]y reworking events that have only received a thorough documentation from the white perspective, [Parks] not only calls into question the validity of this traditional historiography, but also destabilizes and deconstructs the content of this documentation" (2002, 5). Parks creates new historical events by exhuming disappeared materials of the past and bringing them to life in performance.

Parks's interest in performative historiography emerges sharply in *The America Play*, where the Foundling Father (or The Lesser Known), a gravedigger, impersonates Abraham Lincoln because he has been told that he resembles the "Great Man." He begins his career by delivering the Great Man's speeches and creates an arcade booth where customers can pay a penny to simulate Lincoln's assassination, which the Foundling Father performs repeatedly. Initially, he and his family reside in a great hole – the play's primary setting, which Parks describes as "[a] great hole. In the middle of nowhere. The hole is an exact replica of The Great Hole of History" (1995c, 158). Eventually, he leaves his family to venture out west to dig a replica of the great hole of history. His son, Brazil, continues digging, discovering vestiges of the past and placing them in the Hall of Wonders, a museum-like venue. After the Foundling Father's death, his wife, Lucy, and Brazil place his body inside the Hall of Wonders, which is housed within the great hole.

During the play's premiere at the Yale Repertory Theatre (1994), the floor was coated with gravel rather than dirt. Designer, Riccardo Hernandez, had "dreamed up a gleaming white environment with a black-gravel floor suggestive of some vast spectral museum" (Taylor 1994, 70). Parks, however, found the production too sanitized and wished it had been dirtier. She stated that representing the great hole of history as a "vast, glossy, empty whitespace" undermined her intentions "by emphasizing the theoretical over the theatrical" (Garrett 2000, 133). Some productions, such as the 2006 iteration at the Boston Court Theatre in Pasadena, have taken a dirtier approach by "transform[ing] the stage into a black hole, complete with thick mounds of dirt from proscenium to back wall" (Verini 2006).

Scenic designer, James Ogden,[2] wanted the dirt to be as literal as possible for the 2015 production he designed at the Oracle in Chicago. The Oracle was a tiny storefront theatre; so, the dirt presented dilemmas from a production standpoint. "I think the stage [was] like 17-wide by 20 feet deep you know… and then there's audience," recalls Ogden (2021). Ogden explained that the dirt dries out and gets very dusty (2021). It then needs to be watered down, which gets very messy in a small performance space. He elucidated that dirt is "very heavy and … the [theatre] floor was not… structurally sound enough to accommodate [the]… weight [of] … like 2000 pounds of soil or something" (2021). Rather than actual dirt, Ogden decided to use ground cork because it was light and less dusty. He acknowledged the cork was not his first choice but admitted that it looked more beautiful on stage than he expected, particularly when it was activated by the actors. He designed the space to look like a mineshaft, enabling the actors to dig into the "dirt," and pull up "floorboards." He recounted how the actor playing the Foundling Father would have "little moments playing around in the dirt and … diving under the under the floorboards and popping up with something … [and this activation of the 'dirt'] took it to a whole new level" (2021). While literal dirt was not feasible for this production, Ogden utilized cork in a way that still conveyed the significance of soil in the play.

Alternatively, other productions of the play have focused more on physical and metaphorical approaches. For example, a 2019 production at Georgia

State University's Perimeter College directed by Anastasia Wilson[3] focused on the physicality of digging the soil (Wilson 2021). Wilson was concerned that the spectacle of dirt on stage might take away from the story (2021). Instead, she focused on the actor's movements to communicate the exhaustive nature of repetitive digging. To create a space with depth for digging, she inverted the performance space. The backstage space was converted to the seating area, so spectators watched the performance from behind the stage, rather than in front. This positioned the actors further back onto the apron of the stage, which was an orchestra pit. The orchestra pit opened and became the earth into which the characters descended. Wilson explained that using the orchestra pit to create the earth's strata enabled the actors to understand the corporeality of the digging. By descending into and climbing out of the pit, they experienced "the exhaustion [of] ... having to toil with soil, toil with their environment" (Wilson 2021). Wilson specifically worked with the actor playing the Foundling Father on his physicality. She recalls giving him a "heavy shovel" because he had to "understand how [the shovel sits] in your body" (2021). "It exhausted him by the end," she recalls (2021). While literal dirt did not feature in this production, Wilson still focused on significance of the depth of the earth and the physicality of digging.

Movement Generates Meaning

As Wilson's production exhibits, digging is an important recurring movement on stage, as well as a crucial trope in the text. Throughout Act One, the Foundling Father digs his reproduction of the great hole of history, an act he has been performing his entire life as he comes from a family of "diggers":

> THE FOUNDLING FATHER AS ABRAHAM LINCOLN. The Lesser Known was a Digger by trade. From a family of Diggers. Digged graves. He was known in Small Town to dig his graves quickly and neatly. This brought him a steady business.
> (1995c, 160)

Over the course of the play, he digs hundreds of holes. "When the Lesser Known left to find his way out West he figured he had dug over 7 hundred and 23 graves. 7 hundred and 23," the Foundling Father explains (1995c, 169). Years of performing such distinct, repetitive, physical labor shapes his body. According to dance scholar Susan Leigh Foster, the action of executing a specific movement is a form of communication that creates meaning; "A body, whether sitting writing or standing thinking or walking talking or running screaming, is a bodily writing. Its habits and stances, gestures and demonstrations ... all... emerge out of cultural practices ... that construct corporeal meaning" (1995, 3). Moving bodies create meaning. And yet a body's physical movements are shaped through social and cultural practices that exist within established systems of power. Such systems prohibit certain bodies from performing actions in particular spaces or force them to perform other actions. How and why bodies move proves significant in determining the meaning of their motions. When movements are repetitive or performed daily, this performance reveals information about power dynamics as well as social and cultural practices. Foster further explains that "bodily writing" must be understood within aesthetic, political, and historical contexts as "each body's distinctive pronouncements at a given moment must be read against the inscription, along with others, it continuously produces. A blank stare does not mean the same thing for all bodies in all contexts" (1995, 5). A person's movement must be understood in relation to situated and intersectional aspects of their identity, such as race, class, gender, ability, and broader historical and cultural contexts. These aspects and others intersect to cause degrees of privilege or oppression which affect both the body's movement and the potential ways it can be read. Individual movements do not have universal meaning. In the case of the Foundling Father, his repetitive digging can be understood in relation to his race and class within the specific historical and cultural context of white supremacy in the United States. Through his movement, Parks evokes the repetitive labor of enslaved Africans and African Americans who, through the chattel slavery system in the antebellum United States, were forced to work perpetually. Reading the Foundling Father's body and movement in this context exhibits the racialization of these bodies (both the Foundling Father's and the enslaved) and how racialization shapes movement, physicality, and spatiality.

According to feminist scholar Sara Ahmed, racialization is "a process of *investing* skin colour with meaning," and is both discursive and embodied (2002, 46). While racialized bodies are discursively constructed and produced through colonial systems of power, Ahmed emphasizes that it is critical to consider how those constructions affect lived experiences. The racialization of bodies through these systems of power shapes both social and corporeal movement. Ahmed asserts:

> racialization takes place though spatial and tactile negotiations; through different ways of touching and being touched by others, and different ways of inhabiting space with others, boundaries are established between bodies… In racist encounters, the white subject also aligns itself with other white bodies, as closer to them, and against other black bodies, as further away from them. Indeed, different bodies come to be lived through the very habits and gestures of marking out bodily space…into familiar (assimilable, touchable) and strange (unassimilable, untouchable).
> (2002, 60–61)

Social boundaries are established through geographical and kinesthetic movements, being near or far from something. Racialization and racism are established through both large-scale and minute "bodily writing," as people and groups with power determine what spaces are permissible for specific bodies. For enslaved Africans and African Americans in the antebellum United States, settler colonial, white supremacist systems of power regulated and limited the spaces that they were allowed to inhabit. These spatial strictures in turn shaped their kinesthetic movement which in turn shaped their corporeality. Some exhumed remains recovered from the African Burial site in Manhattan exhibit the impacts of this labor on bodies. A display at the memorial identifies how manual labor impacted the skeletal remains. A man's skull was found with a "thickened ridge where his shoulder and neck muscles connected to the back of his head"; this is thought to be "caused by heavy lifting" (Rothstein 2010). While this skull is only a small remain of the impact of manual labor on enslaved people, it exhibits the physical consequences of racialization on a body. The Foundling Father's repetitive manual labor in the dirt can be read in context of these discursive and lived experiences of racism and racialization. His physicality is shaped through the specificity of repetitive digging and thus generates meaning. But exactly how is the Foundling Father's body creating meaning? To consider how bodies produce knowledge, Foster queries what type of body and what kind of movement is being executed:

> Empowered bodies? enslaved bodies? docile bodies? rebellious bodies? dark bodies? pale bodies? exotic bodies? virtuoso bodies? feminine bodies? masculine bodies? triumphant bodies? disappeared bodies? All these genres of bodies first began moving through their days performing what they had learned how to do: carrying, climbing, standing, sitting, greeting, eating, dressing, sleeping, touching, laboring, fighting.... These quotidian activities... these bodies' mundane habits and miniscule gestures mattered ... All a body's characteristic ways of moving resonated with aesthetic and political values.
> (1995, 4–5)

For Foster, the knowledge generated from a moving body is informed by politics and aesthetics. I contend that the Foundling Father's bodily movement is not only a generative dramatic device to evoke the repetitive labor of the enslaved; the act of digging also produces meaning in relation to the history of environmental racism and white supremacy in the United States. These systems generated racialized and racist correlations between Blackness and dirt, and enslavement and the soil, that had material consequences.

Historian Winthrop D. Jordan considers the association between Blackness and dirt. He remarks that, before the 16th century, a definition of "black" in the *Oxford English Dictionary* included "deeply stained with dirt; soiled, filthy, begrimed" (1968, 7). "Embedded in this concept of blackness was its direct opposite – whiteness," asserts Jordan: "White and black connoted purity and filthiness, virginity and sin, virtue and baseness, beauty and ugliness, beneficence and evil, God and the devil" (1968, 7). This destructive dichotomy, used to justify racism, has tangible effects on both bodies and land. Using dirt as a lens to analyze the history of environmental racism in the United States, environmental historian Carl A. Zimring argues that its current manifestations can trace their origins back to the antebellum era. He contends:

> Increasing scientific definitions of waste as hazard and of racial categories in the immediate antebellum period established a foundation for later racist constructions that posited that white people were somehow cleaner than non-white people. This assumption defined white supremacist thinking. Its evolution shaped environmental inequalities that endure in the twenty-first century.
>
> (2015, 3)

The spurious correlations between Blackness and dirt/filth and whiteness and cleanliness/purity heightened during the antebellum era as "physical and moral ills [and] disease [were] linked to soil, mud, and murky water" (Zimring 2015, 3). People associated with these elements were considered not only "dirty" but also disease-ridden and immoral. Here, dirt functions as "matter out of place" (Douglas 1966, 40) and is threatening to the social order because of its potential to pollute or contaminant anything it contacts. Associating dirt with non-whiteness and Blackness situates specific people as "out of place" or "threatening to the social order." As Ahmed explains, in racist encounters social spaces are shaped. White bodies align themselves with other white bodies, distancing themselves from Black bodies, designating them as undesirable and unwelcome in that space (2002). Meaning is generated through the ways in which Black bodies were coded as "dirty" which racialized not only bodies, but also the spaces they inhabited, and ultimately maintained white supremacy.

Affiliation with dirt not only racialized bodies in specific ways but working with the soil also brought about class implications. Historically, many enslaved people in the United States had a complex relationship with the soil in which they labored. Performance studies scholar E. Patrick Johnson explains:

> Since our arrival on American soil, African Americans have always been marked by our class position. Although we were considered only three-fifths human and had no material possessions to speak of, enslaved Africans' intracultural relations were shaped by class, for white masters understood the psychosocial dynamics of divide and conquer: give one group access to the master's house and family and put the other in the fields and forbid them access to the same. Thus the distinction between house slaves and field slaves paradoxically codified a caste system that effectively divided a people along class lines.
>
> (2011, xiii)

Soil functioned as a means to divide enslaved people into two classes. Those working in the field were considered lower class because "[d]irt was seen as primitive and chaotic," whereas those working in a house were of a higher class because "cleanliness ... promised morality, good order and reform" (Ashenburg 2007, 210). Here, dirt operates as a manifestation of labor, and its presence on bodies marks them as uncivilized, low-class, and immoral. It therefore became a signifier of class. Interdisciplinary scholar Anne McClintock expounds, "Smeared on trousers, faces, hands and aprons, dirt was the memory trace of working class and female labor, unseemly evidence that the fundamental production of industrial and imperial wealth lay in the hands and bodies of the working class, women and the colonized" (1995, 154). Dirt, now an indication of disease and immorality, was equated with certain races (those considered not white) and classes. It marked particular bodies as "other," signaling that they should be avoided.

In *The America Play*, Parks returns to this historically fraught relationship with dirt and soil, but she reimagines the relationship with a Black gravedigger, dressed as Lincoln, returning to the land to disinter the detritus. The Foundling Father's occupation and corporeality as a gravedigger embodies the racialization of those associated with dirt and echoes the physical toil of the enslaved who worked on the land. His digging emphasizes those whose lives and identity were in the soil, those who were considered the lowest class even among the oppressed. Regarding these supposed class markers, Johnson notes, "The irony, of course, is that those slaves who were assigned to the plantation home were actually no better off than those in the fields in terms of what they actually had materially. […] Nonetheless this division of labor created an image of what we now call the black middle class that remains today" (2011, xiv). Enslaved people who labored in a house or on the land were not different in terms of their material possessions, but their differences lay in how they were treated by those who enslaved them, which in turn often affected how they treated each other. Enslavers were successful in creating a performance of class that was based on a relationship with the soil. Those who worked in and with the soil were literally treated like dirt, an expendable commodity and contaminant. It was not until 1868, with the adoption of the Fourteenth Amendment, that individuals born or naturalized in the United States were considered American citizens, including those formerly enslaved. While this was one step toward a more equal future, the racialized signifiers and class markers put into place by enslavers persisted. Former enslaved people still faced violent racism as well as racial and class discrimination. African American studies scholar Vershawn Ashanti Young considers the African American struggle for "full class citizenship," stating that "changes in African Americans' experience of citizenship have something, if not everything, to do with the reason that class is now believed by some to be the factor that determines race" (2001, 3). American soil played a part in creating this class system, the effects of which still resound in contemporary culture.

32 Performative Taphonomy

The Foundling Father repeatedly digging into the soil not only invokes a kinesthetic embodiment of enslaved labor but is also a reminder that environmental racism persists, and Black bodies are often still racialized in white spaces.

Activist and scholar, bell hooks, however, offers a counterpoint to the affiliation between soil and enslavement, establishing soil as a space of Black liberation and resistance. Examining the relationship between Southern Black folks and the earth in the 19th century, she argues, "We were indeed a people of the earth. Working the land was the hope of survival. Even when that land was owned by white oppressors ... it was the earth itself that protected exploited black folks from dehumanization" (2002, 68). As hooks explains, even though white enslavers thought they owned the land, ultimately, the earth cannot be controlled as eventually everyone has to submit to the forces of nature. The knowledge that white people did not control the earth offered hope for Black people and established soil as a place of resistance. "This relationship to the earth meant that southern black folks... knew first hand that white supremacy, with is systemic dehumanization of blackness was not a form of absolute power," affirms hooks; "[it] helped imbue black folks with an oppositional sensibility" (2002, 69). She contends that because the earth functioned as a place of opposition, "Reclaiming our history, our relationship to nature, to farming in America ... is meaningful resistance" (2002, 70). hooks's argument enables a reading of the Foundling Father's movement as a means of dissent. While white systems of power were successful in creating racist and classist hierarchies in relation to dirt and soil, these elements were also a reminder that nature cannot be controlled by (white) humans. The Foundling Father's connection with the earth can be read as resistance to colonial power structures. His digging resurrects "bones" that decenter the white historical narrative. In the next section, I examine how the Foundling Father's embodiment of Lincoln, coupled with his corporeal relationship with the soil, enables him to *become* Lincoln in the affective sense, creating a space where history can be "reterritorialized."

Becoming Lincoln

The Foundling Father fashions his physical appearance after Lincoln because he has been told that he resembles him: "everywhere out West he went people remarked on his likeness to Lincoln ... [He] was identical to the Great Man in gait and manner how his legs were long and torso short" (1995c, 163–164). Literature scholar Jennifer Larson explains that embodying Lincoln "[helps] 'The Lesser Known' feel connected to Abraham Lincoln both ideologically and temporally" (2012, 58). In fact, the Foundling Father not only resembles Lincoln but also begins re-enacting Lincoln's assassination for customers:

THE FOUNDLING FATHER AS ABRAHAM LINCOLN:

[W]hen someone remarked that he played Lincoln so well that he ought to be shot, it was as if the Great Mans footsteps had been suddenly revealed:

(Rest) The Lesser Known returned to his hole and, instead of speeching, his act would now consist of a single chair, a rocker, in a dark box. The public was invited to pay a penny, choose from the selection of provided pistols, enter the darkened box and "Shoot Mr. Lincoln." The Lesser Known became famous overnight.

(1995c, 164)

The Foundling Father replicates the corporeality of Lincoln before, during, and after his assassination. He takes this relationship even further by articulating his desire to dig Lincoln's grave, stating that "if he had been in the slightest vicinity back then, [he] would have had at least a chance at the great honor of digging the Great Mans grave" (1995c, 161). He fantasizes about Lincoln's wife summoning him, crying, "*Emergency* oh, *Emergency*, please put the Great Man in the ground" (1995c, 160, italics in original).[4] His desire to perform this task evokes powerful imagery. Dressed as Lincoln, he digs Lincoln's grave, unearthing deeper soil and therefore deeper history, as lower layers of soil can range anywhere from 10,000 to 144 million years old (McCaulay Land Use Research Institute n.d., 14). As he digs Lincoln's grave, the very nature of the soil changes. In its displacement, the soil becomes dirt. Through this biogeocultography, the Foundling Father affects the soil, potentially even unearthing particulates of Lincoln's remains or organic matter that grew out of his decomposing body. And the soil concomitantly affects him as he disinters buried remains that reveal the permeability of material and discursive formations. Through his embodiment of Lincoln, the simulation of Lincoln's death, his grave-digging fantasy, and the biogeocultography of the soil, the Foundling Father and the discursive body of Lincoln develop an affective relationship.

Anthropologist Kathleen Stewart describes affect as,

a surging, a rubbing, a connection of some kind that has an impact. It's transpersonal or prepersonal – not about one person's feelings becoming another's but about bodies literally affecting one another and generating intensities: human bodies, discursive bodies, bodies of thought, bodies of water.

(2007, 128)

Affect, then, is an exchange of intensities that physically and metaphysically alter the bodies engaged in the transfer; it has the potential to modify or transform the bodies involved. Deleuze uses the terms "deterritorialization" and "reterritorialization" to describe how physical and immaterial states are altered when two or more bodies enter an affective relationship (1993, 33). This restructuring of the territory of "self" enables bodies to physically and metaphysically change as they exchange intensities and particles that recompose their forms. Through his embodiment, movement, and relationship with the soil, the Foundling Father is affected by the historical narrative of Lincoln and, in return, affects the narrative himself. By taking on the physicality and aesthetics of Lincoln, re-enacting crucial moments in his life, and surrounding himself with the material detritus in the soil (perhaps comprising Lincoln's remains), the Foundling Father's body is deterritorialized. He and the discursive body of Lincoln are reterritorialized, altering both their forms and creating a space where alternative narratives of the past can be explored. The Foundling Father becomes Lincoln to understand the present through the past (or the past through the present). Through this relationship, Parks imagines a reterritorialization of Black bodies, Abraham Lincoln, and the historical narrative of the United States. She tinkers with the narrative to explore alternate possibilities and imaginings of those "facts." For example, the Foundling Father offers a range of Lincoln assassination experiences. Some simulations are based on historical "accuracy," while others are devised from rumors. He has a particular customer who comes in once a week and re-creates the event exactly how it is recorded in history books:

> THE FOUNDLING FATHER: Comes once a week that one. Always chooses the Derringer although we've got several styles he always chooses the Derringer. Always "The tyrants" and then "The South avenged." The ones who choose the Derringer are the ones for History. He's one for History. As it Used to Be. Never wavers. No frills. By the book. Nothing excessive.
>
> (1995c, 166)

Some customers do not deviate from the recorded narrative. But others change the events to suit their own purposes, such as the newlywed couple who wants to shoot the Foundling Father together:

> C MAN: You allow 2 at once?
> THE FOUNDLING FATHER:
>   (Rest)
> C WOMAN: We're just married. You know: newlyweds. We hope you
>   dont mind. Us both at once.
> THE FOUNDLING FATHER:
>   (Rest)
> C MAN: We're just married.
> C WOMAN: Newlyweds.
> THE FOUNDLING FATHER:
>   (Rest)
>   (Rest)
>   (They "stand in position." Both hold one gun).
>
> (1995c, 169–170)

Some deviations cannot be appreciated by customers, such as the Foundling Father's fancy yellow beard. He explains, "Mr. Lincolns hair was dark so I dont wear it much. If you deviate too much they wont get their pleasure. Thats my experience. Some inconsistencies are perpetuatable because theyre good for business" (1995c, 163). On the other hand, some deviations are "good for business," such as the stovepipe hat, which as the Foundling Father notes, Lincoln "[never] really [wore] indoors but people dont like their Lincoln hatless" (1995c, 168).

The interactions between the Foundling Father and his customers illustrate that those who record, interpret, and perform history allow for some leeway in their narratives, but not too much. Once you begin to deviate too far from the "facts," consumers become uncomfortable because they want pleasure and familiarity in their history. By drawing attention to the arbitrary lines of historical "truth," Parks emphasizes the history and historicity of events, demonstrating Hutcheon's claim that "the meaning and shape are not *in the events*, but *in the systems* which make those past 'events' into present historical 'facts'" (1988, 89, italics in original). While Parks plays with notions of history and historicity in the Foundling Father's simulation of Lincoln's death, she takes this further in his relationship with the hole of history. Through his embodiment of Lincoln and the biogeocultography of his perpetual digging in the soil (the hole of history), Parks reimagines the past to conceive of a different present and future.

Putting the Body Back Together

In *What is Philosophy*? Deleuze and Guattari detail the differences between philosophy and science. Philosophy explores the virtual, the range of potentials and possibilities that something can become. Science, on the other hand, deals with actualization; it explores the materialization of the virtual into "states of affairs" (Deleuze and Guattari 1994, 122). Philosophy is composed of concepts that reside on the plane of immanence, which is "the breath that suffuses the separate parts" and connects the concepts to one another, a site of virtual possibilities (Deleuze and Guattari 1994, 36). As Deleuze and Guattari explain, "[c]oncepts are events, but the plane is the horizon of events, the reservoir or reserve of purely conceptual events" (1994, 36). The virtual possibilities (concepts) that reside on the plane of immanence have the potential to become actualized "states of affairs." This actualization occurs when the "states of affairs" and virtual events, which are located on two different vectors, intersect. At the moment of intersection an event is actualized: the concept moves from the virtual (the world of philosophy) to the actual (the world of science); the concept becomes concretized in time and space. Regarding this process, Deleuze and Guattari assert:

> [T]he state of affairs actualizes a chaotic virtuality by carrying along with it a space that has ceased, no doubt, to be virtual but that still shows its

origin and serves as absolutely indispensable correlate to the state of affairs ... *A state of affairs cannot be separated from the potential through which it takes effect.*

(1994, 153, italics in original)

While the "state of affairs" has actualized, it still contains the initial concept, the virtual possibility, as the two cannot be severed.

Deleuze and Guattari's theory is generative in relation to *The America Play* because Parks explores history and historicity by experimenting with recorded and possible events. She takes people and events that have been actualized, like Lincoln and his assassination, and uses the Foundling Father's digging as a taphonomic method of inquiry to explore the virtual possibilities of what could have been. She moves from the scientific realm of "states of affairs" to the philosophical realm of concepts to explore what other virtual possibilities resided on the plane of immanence, what other events had the potential to occur. In other words, she disregards the linear Hegelian timeline imposed on history and uses a philosophic lens to view events differently. "Time has a circular shape," writes Parks: "Could Time be tricky like the world once was – looking flat from our place on it – and through looking at things beyond the world we found it round?" (1995a, 10). Through the Foundling Father digging the great hole, Parks explores what circular time might look like. "The relationships between whole and hole, time and space, history and Lincoln, are at once logical and illogical, sequential and nonsequential," explain drama scholars Harry Elam and Alice Rayner (1999, 181). Parks demonstrates this understanding of time when the Foundling Father discusses trying to "catch up" with Lincoln:

THE FOUNDLING FATHER: The Great Man lived in the past that is was an inhabitant of time immemorial and the Lesser Known out West alive a resident of the present. And the Great Mans deeds had transpired during the life of the Great Man somewhere in past-land that is somewhere "back there" and all this while the Lesser Known digging his holes bearing the burden of his resemblance all the while trying somehow to equal the Great Man in stature, word and deed going forward with his lesser life trying somehow to follow in the Great Mans footsteps that were of course behind him. The Lesser Known trying somehow to catch up to the Great Man all this while and maybe running too fast in the wrong direction. Which is to say that maybe the Great Man had to catch him.

(1995c, 170–171)

The Foundling Father tries to follow in the Great Man's footsteps, which he recognizes are not ahead of but behind him. He concedes that perhaps he is trying to move in the wrong direction and that perhaps it is the Great Man who needs to catch up with him. In this monologue, as in the entire play, Parks plays with conventional notions of time and space and looks to virtual possibilities or concepts, the "paths not taken," to explore what could have been or what still might be.

By setting the play in a replica of the great hole of history, including both the history that was recorded and the history that was left out, Parks toys with the historical narrative. She places a Black gravedigger dressed as Lincoln disinterring the soil, transferring particles of the past into the present, an act that imagines an alternative history. As the Foundling Father digs, new "bones" emerge, revealing the fragmented and incomplete nature of history. In Act Two, his son, Brazil, encouraged by his mother, Lucy, continues to dig: "Dig on, Brazil. Cant stop diggin till you dig up somethin" (1995c, 174). Encountering an artifact "might confirm the materiality of the past, if not its meaning," assert Elam and Rayner (1999, 184). Therefore, Lucy tells Brazil he can't stop looking for the material remains that have been erased. She has given him the responsibility of searching for the discarded fragments, telling him, "Go on: dig. Now me I need tuh know thuh real thing from thuh echo. Thuh truth from thuh hearsay" (1995c, 175). Lucy needs to know the truth; she is not satisfied with what has been written down, so she compels Brazil to dig on.

The (white) narrative of American history often fails to account for the experiences of African Americans because their stories have been violently omitted, or as Parks puts it, "unrecorded, dismembered, washed out" (1995b, 4). *The America Play* therefore serves as an archaeological project in which the Foundling Father and later Brazil dig to unearth the past. When the Foundling Father descends into the hole, he is inserting something from the present (his body) directly into the past (the soil) and transferring something from the past (the deeper soil) into the present (the surface). His biogeocultography displaces the soil and exhumes material remains. The plantation soil where enslaved people labored, which dictated their status, is the same soil that exists today; it is simply covered by more recent history. Thus, the strata into which the Foundling Father digs is not neutral.

As a scholar of inhuman geography, Kathryn Yusoff argues, "geology is a racial formation built on the labor of Black and Indigenous peoples who were categorized, by white, colonial systems of power, as inhuman matter" (2018, 6).[5] Countering the white geology of the Anthropocene, Yusoff examines how the processes and practices that created this epoch are both a product of and reinforce colonialism. She contends that "through a universalist geologic commons... the Anthropocene ... neatly erases histories of racism that were incubated through the regulatory structure of geologic relations" (Yusoff 2018, 2, italics in original). As Native American cultural studies scholar Kali Simmons (Oglala Lakota) explains, the origins of the Anthropocene are grounded in racialization, enslavement, and extractive imperialism, which are evinced through the Orbis Spike, "an indexical mark of colonial violence upon the Earth itself" (2019, 176).[6] The Orbis Spike materialized from the severe drop in atmospheric carbon generated from "the population decline of the Americas from around sixty million to six million due to colonial war, famine, disease, and enslavement" (Simmons 2019, 175–176). This is not an apolitical origin story, but rather evidence of how "coloniality and anti-Blackness are materially inscribed into the Anthropocene" (Yusoff 2018, 19). The very stratum of the earth comprises the bodies and extracted labor of people who were categorized as inhuman matter. Thus, excavating and exhuming the soil are not neutral actions. The Foundling Father and Brazil's digging are political acts of resistance (per hooks's argument), as they unearth and bear witness to the discarded remains created through extractive imperialist systems.

Performance studies scholar Dwight Conquergood discusses how performance functions as kinesis, "movement, motion, fluidity, fluctuation, all those restless energies that transgress boundaries and trouble closure" (1995, 138). He cites Homi K. Bhabha's definition of performative as an "action that incessantly insinuates, interrupts, interrogates, antagonizes, and decenters powerful master discourse" and argues that performance ultimately has the power to break and remake (Conquergood 1995, 138). Movement can be performative; it has the power to "do" something. As Conquergood argues, it can permeate borders, dismantle master narratives, and create new and different modes of understanding; it has the power to reterritorialize discourse. If this logic is extended to *The America Play*, the Foundling Father's digging, evoking the labor of enslaved people, is a political act that disturbs the white geology of the Anthropocene by searching for and exhuming material remains. He executes a performative taphonomy that "interrupts, interrogates, antagonizes" (Conquergood 1995, 138), the canonized (settler-colonial) version of the United States' history. The Foundling Father searches for disappeared Black bodies and materials of Black labor. He excavates and exhumes them and "rewrit[es] the Time Line" (Parks 1995b, 5). The Foundling Father dismantles master narratives by unearthing conceptual possibilities on the plane of immanence that create space for alternate histories. His disinterment of soil enacts a biogeocultography that reterritorializes history.

History is a discourse, and the constructed narrative is incomplete. Parks addresses the fragmentary nature of history in the margins of her essay "Possession." She writes:

> memory
> un-remembered
> dis-membered
> re-member
> "his bones cannot
> be found"
> putting the body
> back together
>
> (Parks 1995b, 5).

These words poetically communicate the permeability of person and place, individual and ecological community, that the body of history is disassembled. And yet the past is present in the soil. To unearth dirt is to bring history to the surface. To exhume the "un-remembered," "dis-membered" bones is to begin to "re-member," creating "memory" and, in doing so, beginning to put the body of history back together. The Foundling Father performs a biogeocultography through his digging, uncovering material and discursive possibilities that are buried in the soil. This movement generates a performative taphonomy, as the exhumed materials exhibit the intersections of social and environmental injustice. As he continues to dig for disappeared material, he gives voice to the "un-remembered," "dis-membered" stories and begins to reassemble the historical narrative (Parks 1995b, 5). History is a narrative fashioned by those with power. Should we be content with incomplete narratives when fragments of the past lie buried beneath the soil, awaiting disinterment?

The next chapter focuses on the materiality of the peat used in Pina Bausch's adaptation of *The Rite of Spring* (1975). An exploration of the biological composition, environmental significance, and historical implications of peat demonstrates that its use in *The Rite of Spring* conveys distinct meanings that are situated in its geographical and cultural contexts. The peat's presence in this production stages a rupture that exposes the extractive logics of capitalism that contribute to climate change and erase history.

Notes

1 For more information about the African Burial Ground, visit the website through the National Parks Service (2022), http://www.nps.gov/afbg/index.htm.
2 James Ogden is a scenic designer and visual artist.
3 Anastasia Wilson is an actor, devising artist, and Flamenco dancer. For more information about her work, see her website, https://www.anastasia-wilson.com/.
4 A footnote in the play indicates that these were "[p]ossibly the words of Mary Todd Lincoln after the death of her husband" (1995, 160), but Parks admitted in an interview that most of the footnotes are "totally made up and ridiculous" (Pearce 1994, 26). In other words, the playwright constructs her own history as surely as the Foundling Father does.
5 For Yusoff, inhuman matter renders "subjects not as persons... but as a commodity with properties... without subjective will or agency" (2018, 6).
6 The Orbis Spike is a specific Golden Spike. Golden Spikes are the proposed marks in the earth's strata that demonstrate an epoch shift, e.g., from the Holocene to the Anthropocene.

References

Ahmed, Sara. 2002. "Racialized Bodies." In *Real Bodies*, edited by Mary Evans and Ellie Lee, 46–63. London: Palgrave.
Ashenburg, Katherine. 2007. *The Dirt on Clean: An Unsanitized History*. New York: North Point.

Chang, Ailsa. 2020. "The Story of A Memorial: The African Burial Ground in New York," NPR's All Things Considered transcript. July 16, 2020. Accessed June 23, 2021. https://www.npr.org/2020/07/16/892034381/the-story-of-a-memorial-the-african-burial-ground-in-new-york.

Conquergood, Dwight. 1995. "Of caravans and carnivals: Performance studies in motion." *TDR* 39, no. 4: 137–141.

Deleuze, Gilles. 1993. "Rhizome Versus Trees." In *The Deleuze Reader*, edited by Constantin V. Boundas. New York: Columbia University Press.

Deleuze, Gilles and Félix Guattari. 1994. *What is Philosophy?* Trans. Hugh Tomlinson and Graham Burchell. New York: Columbia University Press.

Douglas, Mary. 1966. *Purity and Danger: An Analysis of Concepts of Pollution and Taboo*. London: Routledge.

Elam, Harry and Alice Rayner. 1999. "Echoes from the Black (W)hole: An Examination of *The America Play* by Suzan-Lori Parks." In *Performing America: Cultural Nationalism in American Theater*, edited by Jeffrey D. Mason and J. Ellen Gainor, 178–192. Ann Arbor: University of Michigan Press.

Foster, Susan Leigh. 1995. "An Introduction to Moving Bodies." In *Choreographing History*, edited by Susan Leigh Foster, 3–24. Bloomington: Indiana University Press.

Frank, Haike. 2002. "The Instability of Meaning in Suzan-Lori Parks's The America Play." *American Drama* 11, no. 2: 4–20.

Garrett, Shawn-Marie. 2000 "The Possession of Suzan-Lori Parks." *American Theatre* 17, no. 8: 22–32.

hooks, bell. 2002. "Earthbound on Solid Ground." In *The Colors of Nature*, edited by Alison H. Deming and Lauret E. Savoy, 67–71. Minneapolis: Milkweed Editions.

Hutcheon, Linda. 1988. *A Poetics of Postmodernism: History, Theory, Fiction*. London: Routledge.

Johnson, E. Patrick. 2011. "Foreword: The Journey from Bourgeois to Boojie." *In From Bourgeois to Boojie: Black Middle Class Performance*, edited by Vershawn Ashanti Young and Bridget Harris Tsemo, xiii–xxv. Detroit: Wayne State University Press.

Jordan, Winthrop D. 1968. *White Over Black: American Attitudes toward the Negro, 1550–1812*. Chapel Hill: University of North Carolina Press.

Larson, Jennifer. 2012. *Understanding Suzan-Lori Parks*. Columbia: University of South Carolina Press.

Martin, Ronald E. 1999. *Taphonomy: A Process Approach*. Cambridge: Cambridge University Press.

McCaulay Land Use Research Institute. n.d. "The Soil Beneath Your Feet – Where Does It Come From?" The James Hutton Institute, n.d., 11. Accessed August 2017. http://www.macaulay.ac.uk/soilquality/soil_beneath_feet.pdf.

McClintock, Anne. 1995. *Imperial Leather: Race, Gender and Sexuality in the Colonial Contest*. New York: Routledge.

McKittrick, Katherine. 2013. "Plantation futures." *Small Axe: A Caribbean Journal of Criticism* 17, no. 3 (42): 1–15.

National Park Service. 2021. "History and Culture." Last updated November 23, 2022. Accessed August 12, 2022. https://www.nps.gov/afbg/learn/historyculture/index.htm.

National Park Service. 2022. "African Burial Ground." Last updated September 23, 2023. Accessed August 12, 2022. http://www.nps.gov/afbg/index.htm.

Ogden, James. Interview (virtual) by Angenette Spalink. Zoom. Bryan, Texas. July 7, 2021.

Parks, Suzan-Lori. 1995a. "Elements of Style." In *The America Play and Other Works*, 6–18. New York: Theatre Communications Group.

Parks, Suzan-Lori. 1995b. "Possession." In *The America Play and Other Works*, 3–5. New York: Theatre Communications Group.

Parks, Suzan-Lori. 1995c. "The America Play" In *The America Play and Other Works*, 157–199. New York: Theatre Communications Group.

Pearce, Michele. 1994. "Alien Nation: An Interview with the Playwright." *American Theatre* 11, no. 3: 26.

Rothstein, Edward. 2010. "A Burial Ground and Its Dead Are Given Life." *The New York Times*. February 26, 2010. Accessed July 7, 2021. https://www.nytimes.com/2010/02/26/arts/design/26burial.html.

Simmons, Kali. 2019. "Reorientations: or, An Indigenous Feminist Reflection on the Anthropocene." *Journal of Cinema and Media Studies* 58, no. 2: 174–179.

Stewart, Kathleen. 2007. *Ordinary Affects*. London: Duke University Press.

Taylor, Markland. 1994. "Review of The America Play," by Suzan-Lori Parks, directed by Liz Diamond. *Variety*. Jan.31–Feb. 6, 1994.

Verini, Bob. 2006. "Review of The America Play," by Suzan-Lori Parks, directed by Nancy Keystone. *Variety*. Oct. 23, 2006.

Warner, Sara L. 2008. "Suzan-Lori Parks's Drama of Disinterment: A Transnational Exploration of Venus." *Theatre Journal* 60, no. 2: 181–199.

Wilson, Anastasia. Interview (virtual) by Angenette Spalink. Zoom. Bryan, Texas. July 5, 2021.

Young, Vershawn Ashanti. 2011. "Introduction: Performing Citizenship." In *From Bourgeois to Boojie: Black Middle Class Performance*, edited by Vershawn Ashanti Young and Bridget Harris Tsemo, 1–40. Detroit: Wayne State University Press.

Yusoff, Kathryn. 2018. *A Billion Black Anthropocenes or None*. Minneapolis: University of Minnesota Press.

Zimring, Carl A. 2015. *Clean and White*. New York: New York University Press.

2 Staging Extraction
Peat's Vitality in Pina Bausch's *The Rite of Spring*

A group of stagehands approach six dumpster-sized containers of peat on a bare stage. They knock over the containers and disperse the peat across the floor with brooms, careful to smooth over their footprints so that the peat bears no traces of their movement. Once the peat is evenly distributed across the floor, the stagehands disappear. A dancer appears lying face down on a silky swath of red cloth.[1] She nuzzles her head down into the cloth, undulates her torso and legs, and gently oscillates her right arm through the peat. Another dancer runs into the space. She crouches down in an extreme *grand plié*, extending her knees beyond her feet. Her right hand rests on her left shoulder and her left hand reaches down, clenching fistfuls of peat that spill out between her fingers. Suddenly, the stage is littered with dancers walking, running, and leaping through the peat. Soon, the evenly distributed peat is irregular, marked with inscriptions of the dancers' movements. The dancers' bodies also bear the markings of the movement as they become increasingly coated with peat and sweat as the dance progresses.

This description of *Le Sacre du Printemps* is based on footage captured by Wim Wenders in his documentary, *Pina* (2011), which documents many of German choreographer Pina Bausch's creative works. The film presents scenes from several of Bausch's productions and offers rare glimpses into the handling of the peat used in *Le Sacre du Printemps*. This chapter focuses on the materiality of the human and more-than-human performers in *Le Sacre du Printemps*, translated to English as *The Rite of Spring*. I offer a close reading of the peat that illuminates the complexity of its presence in the performance. Even though it has been displaced, the peat asserts its vitality, demonstrating that it is a performer in its own right. Putting ecocritical theory in conversation with dance scholarship, I argue that the biogeocultography of the peat exhibits an ecological rupture that exposes a multiplicity of ecological matter present in the performance.

History of *The Rite of Spring*

I first present a brief history of *The Rite of Spring* and Bausch's implementation of peat in her adaptation.[2] *The Rite of Spring* (1913) was first staged in Paris at the Ballets Russes by Vaslav Nijinsky with a score composed by Igor Stravinsky. Through dance and music, *The Rite of Spring* tells the story of a young virgin who is selected and sacrificed as part of an annual fertility rite. Once the virgin is chosen, she dances to her death, thereby ensuring the return of spring. Dance historian Joan Cass situates Nijinsky's production choices within the context of Russian folk history:

> Stravinsky's score created the mood both for Nijinsky and for the audience. The composer had set out to create an exciting image of pagan Russia in its annual reawakening from the frozen sleep of winter. His explicit scenario describes an ancient rite of fertility in which tribal elders choose and dedicate the tribe's fairest virgin, who must then dance until she dies of exhaustion ... this sacrifice is intended to ensure fertility, both for the people in the primitive village and for their spring crops.
>
> (1993, 173)

Theatre scholar Erika Fischer-Lichte affirms that the ritual portrayed in *The Rite of Spring* is probably based on an anthropological theory regarding the Spring Demon Ritual. "The dancers represented different groups or members of an ancient Slavic community, celebrating the coming of spring," explains Fischer-Lichte. "The feast ends with a virgin sacrifice: one of the young girls sacrifices herself in a great holy dance, the great sacrifice" (Fischer-Lichte 2005, 65). Such religious festivals and rituals were tied to an agrarian cycle in which seasonal shifts were closely associated with fertility and crops.

Nijinsky's jarring choreography set against Stravinsky's dissonant score created a dynamic and provocative image of this ancient ritual. The choreography challenged traditional notions of classical ballet, which typically featured turn out of the hips, pointe work, symmetry, and graceful, ethereal movements. Nijinsky, instead, had dancers perform with their bodies low to the ground and their feet turned in. "The dancers were seen in strange... quivering motions, with their knees and toes turned in, and their heads leaning sideways on one arm which was in turn supported by the other fist," describes Cass (1993, 173). "Bodies were rigid or bent awkwardly. Groups appeared in a mass, rather than in geometrically clear patterns" (Cass 1993, 173). These grounded, asymmetrical movements would not have been common for the Ballets Russes or the venue at the time. Audiences viewing the production may have been surprised with the break from classical ballet. Stravinsky's score also ventured out of the conventional form. Cass describes it as possessing "striking rhythms of pounding intensity," "complex broken meter," and "bitonal sound" (193, 173). The combination of discordant music with frantic dancing is said to have created an energetic dynamic on stage.

The Rite of Spring has had many incarnations, including adaptations by Mary Wigman (1957), Léonide Massine (1920), Martha Graham (1984), Maurice Béjart (1959), Pina Bausch (1975), and Yang Liping (2018). Each choreographic adaptation illuminates different physical movements and facets of the ritual sacrifice. Concerning the adaptations Cass claims, "[all] of these works dealing with the rite of spring are about ... sacrifice that celebrates the cycle of the year of life. They honor the promise of spring – the season of fertile growth, mating, and the rebirth after the frozen dead of winter" (1993, xi). Even though choreographers have created their own versions, at the core of many productions is the ritual of virgin sacrifice, the spilling of blood into the earth, which must be completed for spring to arrive. When *New York Times* journalist Alan Riding interviewed Bausch about her choreographic process for *The Rite of Spring*, she responded:

> The first thing I did was to talk to them [dancers] about what "Sacre" [rite] means to me.... The starting point is the music. There are so many feelings in it; it changes constantly. There is also much fear in it. I thought, how would it be to dance knowing you have to die? How would you feel, how would I feel? The Chosen One is special, but she dances knowing the end is death. The dancers listened carefully with big ears. They seemed very interested.
> (Riding 1997)

As she indicates in the interview, Bausch's process for *The Rite of Spring* was true to her signature creative method. Grounded in inquiry, her approach elicits choreography from individual dancer's particular emotions and experiences. Discussing Bausch's process, dancer Dominique Mercy remarks,

> She starts with questions. For instance, in the one piece she says; "Tell me what you ate last night," or something to do with Christmas, or six different ways to be sad or angry, and of course with time, because this lasts quite a while, the questions become more complicated. Each time it's always your own experience. Even if you take things from the outside, it's the way you see them. It's yourself which is on stage.
> (Williams 1997, 106)

Drawing on the European expressionist dance traditions of Rudolf Laban, Mary Wigman, and her teacher Kurt Jooss, Bausch creates choreography based on the individual experiences of her performers.[3] She chooses dancers based on their personalities, rather than on their aesthetic or technique. Her process for *The Rite of Spring* began with asking each dancer to consider death in relation to the piece, their personal experiences, and their movement.

First staged in 1975 at the Opera House Wuppertal in Germany, Bausch's adaptation featured Stravinsky's original score and new choreography. In contrast with Nijinsky who situated his staging in Russia, Bausch's production takes place in an unspecified time and location. The production does not use scenic elements; only a layer of peat covers the stage. The male dancers wear pants, while the female dancers wear thin, translucent, beige dresses. The Chosen One (the sacrificial virgin) wears a red, diaphanous dress. As the dancers move, peat flies into the air, sticking to their bodies and costumes. Once the Chosen One is selected, she begins dancing slowly. Her movements build as she works her way into an ecstatic series of movements involving jumping, hunching over, torso contractions, and circular arm motions. As her dancing accelerates, the frenetic movements cause part of her dress to fall to her waist. She continues dancing and the other side of her dress plummets. She gestures down to the earth with her hands and then up to the sky, repeating these movements with fervor until she collapses to her death. The Chosen One's body will eventually decompose and become part of the soil, ensuring the return of spring.

Incorporated into the production by Bausch and scenic designer Rolf Borzik, the peat was not Bausch's first foray into using ecological matter in her work. In other pieces, she incorporates water, grass, leaves, and sand. Expounding on her work with these elements, Bausch expresses that "It's a big joy to dance in the earth ... we can get sweaty, we can have evening dresses get completely wet.... [I]f you walk on the grass it's silent, it's soft, or there are mosquitoes around. It has smell. It has a certain temperature" (Williams 1997, 74). For Bausch, it is about the kinesthetic experience of working with ecological matter. What does it feel like? Smell like? Look like? Sound like? How does it affect the way the body moves through space? The element is a critical aspect of the choreography. Bausch elaborates that "the stage – the settings – are important ... We aren't just dancing in a room, in a space. Where it is, the location, the atmosphere where the movement happens, that matters in my work" (Loney 1985, 97).

For Bausch, environment is not merely a backdrop; it is an integral part of her choreography and composition. While Bausch discusses the joys of using different elements in her work, the way she often utilizes them is not joyful or life affirming. Her implementation of ecological matter is often unnerving, violent, and jarring. Take for instance *Viktor*, where a dancer places bloody strips of raw meat into her pointe shoes. As she dances, blood oozes from her shoes. Or *Nelken*, where dancers perform on a stage that is covered with thousands of carnations. When the dance is completed, most of the carnations have been crushed. In *Gerbirge*, a dancer "drowns" in an expanse of chopped pine trees, their bright green needles suggesting they were recently displaced from a forest (Cody 1998, 127). These are not bodies and nature in harmony, but rather out of context and at odds with one another. Discussing her unsettling use of nature, drama scholar Gabrielle Cody asserts,

> Bausch's necessary cruelty extends to her use of "real" nature, torn from its organic root and bluntly placed in the artificial enclosure of a theatre. This gesture – the mythical rendering of a catastrophic, global displacement – is in and of itself her most powerful metaphor for the fragmentation of our condition through the cultural representation of organic bodies. Such violence can seem tasteless to some.
>
> (1998, 127)

While the excessive use of ecological matter on stage can seem violent and tasteless, Cody argues that Bausch does it purposefully. She contends, "Pina Bausch – a quintessential witness of the postmodern condition, whose pieces are fraught with images of consumerism and waste – may be writing the truest most credible naturalism of our time" (Cody 1998, 129). Bausch's work, featuring displaced and discordant human and more-than-human bodies, is ripe for ecocritical examination.[4] In the next section, I consider the peat's biological composition and environmental history to demonstrate that its significance in *The Rite of Spring* is rooted in its distinct ecological context.

Peat

Bogs are comprised primarily of species in the moss genus *Sphagnum* L. (hereafter, sphagnum). Sphagnum leaves have photosynthetic cells and porous hyaline cells that allow the moss to store about twenty times its weight in water. As the sphagnum decays, it forms peat, "partially decomposed plant remains which form stratified layers" (Curtis 1959, 237). Bogs are typically located throughout North America and Europe with a high density in Germany, Scandinavia, Ireland, and Scotland. Peat's chemical balance and acidic environment make it an excellent preservative of organic material. In "Bog Science" Jarrett A. Lobell and Samir S. Patel explain peats chemical composition:

> Bogs form when moss accumulates in low-lying patches of land. The moss saturates the soil with water and prevents oxygen and nutrients from circulating in. The bacteria normally responsible for the breakdown of organic material cannot function without oxygen, leaving behind a wet, mostly undecomposed mash. The growth of more moss on top continues the cycle, covering old peat with new. This buried organic material breaks down a little and releases a complex and poorly understood cocktail of chemicals, some of which have preservative properties.
>
> (2010b)

Bogs are typically nutrient poor because of sparse decomposition and recycling of elements in the soil. Their unique physical and chemical constitutions make them a hospitable habitat for a vast array of species, including sedges, carnivorous plants, orchids, beetles, and an array of migratory birds (Hancock et al. 2018, 167–178). Peatlands are excellent carbon sinks because they decompose slowly. They accumulate carbon over time and prevent its release into the atmosphere, aiding in the prevention of climate change. While peatlands cover only 3% of the earth's surface, they contain about one quarter of the earth's soil carbon (Gewin 2020).

Because of its capacity to retain carbon, peat is collected as a fuel source in many countries. Farmers harvest it by digging ditches to drain water. Once the water is removed, the peat is left to dry out, eliminating many of its organisms and chemicals. Extracted peat can be found in certain textiles, filters, and gardening products (International Peat Society, n.d.). Burning peat also generates power and heat for commercial and residential purposes (International Peat Society, n.d.). Industrial agriculture has demolished many peatlands. By burning peat, energy producers effectively transform it from a carbon sink into a source of environmental carbon dioxide, the primary greenhouse gas associated with climate change. Drainage and harvesting reduce the acreage of peatlands available to function as carbon sequesters and thus further contribute to an increase in environmental carbon dioxide. According to the International Union for the Conservation of Nature (IUCN), "damaged peatlands contribute about 10% of greenhouse gas emissions from the land use sector" ("Peatlands and Climate Change" n.d.). The extraction of peat and the destruction of peatlands are thus massive contributors to global climate change. Organizations like the Global Peatlands Initiative (GPI) and many grassroots efforts are working to reduce emissions by restoring peatlands and developing more sustainable ways to manage them (GPI 2016). But restoration efforts often have limited success as peat is harvested faster than it can re-grow (approximately 1 mm per year, or 1 inch every 25.4 years).

Not only do the extractive logics underpinning peat harvesting cause ecological damage and climate change, but these practices also destroy material remains. Peat bogs have been preserving bodies and organic matter for thousands for years. The mining of peat exhibits a destruction of the past, for the consumption of energy in the present. Hundreds of human remains have been unearthed in Northwestern Europe that archeologists believe could date back to the Iron Age (500 B.C.–A.D. 100) (Lobell and Patel 2010a). One of the earliest bog bodies discovered in Denmark, the Koelbjerg Woman, is believed to date back to about 8000 B.C. (Lobell and Patel 2010a). Archeologists speculate that many of these remains may be connected to ancient Celtic rituals (Lobell and Patel 2010a). Dr. Anne Ross, an archeologist specializing in Celtic history, conducted research on the "bog body" unearthed in 1984 that became known as the Lindow Man. Her research indicated that the Lindow Man was probably killed as part of a religious Druidic rite (Browne 1988).

The Lindow Man and other preserved remains provide insight into the past. Much like the Foundling Father in *The America Play*, archeologists excavate peat, unearthing fragments to create a more complete historical record. Environmental history "maps human history from the point of view of its ... interface with... the land," explains theatre scholar Theresa J. May (2007, 102). "Thus, it allows us to see how geological and ecological conditions have informed human affairs, and ... how human activities have far-reaching though often occluded effects on environments" (May 2007, 102). The peat not only preserves fragments of human history but also has its own history. When peat is damaged, a variety of intersecting consequences transpire. Not only does its destruction release carbon dioxide into the atmosphere, but it also destroys preserved organic materials that could illuminate the past. The peat's presence in *The Rite of Spring* enacts a biogeocultography as it has been *geographically* transplanted from its environment. This alters the peat's *biology* as it is no longer a carbon sink or material archive. The environmental history of the displaced peat creates biological, geographical, and cultural meaning in the performance, which I explore in the following sections.

The next section, "'Dirty' Dancing," draws from cultural theories of disgust to argue that the peat's inscription on the dancer's bodies is read by dance critic, Arlene Croce, as abject. In "Vital Peat," the section that follows, I theorize the peat through the scholarship of those working within eco-relational and Indigenous frameworks. Through these ontologies, the peat is perceived not as an abject substance, but an animate being. A vital performer in the piece.

"Dirty" Dancing

In the opening scene, a dancer, lying face down in the velvety peat, extends her right arm. She gently opens and closes her hand which causes the peat to accumulate and spill out between her fingers. Four more dancers appear, lying face down in the peat. They begin caressing it with slow curving movements and as they do, the topography of the peat changes. The peat responds to their movements by accumulating on their hands and fingers and forming small piles around their bodies. The peat changes as the sweat, hair, and skin cells of the dancers alter its composition. When the dancers eventually stand up, the peat beneath them is compacted, leaving an impression of their absent bodies – an inverse representation of preserved bog bodies. This scene is a stark contrast to the frenetic, vertical movements that occur later in the piece. In a subsequent scene, the dancers stomp down into the earth, sending clouds of peat into the air. As more and more billows of peat fill the atmosphere, the composition of the dancers change. The peat penetrates their pores and gets matted in their hair. It accumulates on their skin and mingles with their perspiration. Both the dancers and peat are materially altered through their interactions.

As discussed in Chapter 1, bodies and skin are not ahistorical or neutral. They are inscribed through cultural and social structures and thus understood in specific ways based on these contexts. In their work on skin and temporality, cultural studies scholars Sara Ahmed and Jackie Stacey point out that "in consumer culture we are encouraged to read skin, especially feminine skin, as something that needs to be worked upon in order to be protected from the passage of time" (2001, 1). Western conventions of beauty value youthful, smooth, and soft skin. Wrinkles and blemishes are treated as things that need to be "fixed," to conceal the material effects of time on the body. The ways in which skin is marked, stretched, and inscribed (or not) inform how it is constituted and understood in various and situated ways. In *The Rite of Spring*, the peat inscribes the dancers' skin in ways that are read as "dirty" and "disgusting." As the dancers fall, twist, and stomp through the peat, each dancer produces distinct sweat patterns that cause the peat to accrue differently on their skin. Consequently, each dancer becomes a unique composition of sweat, peat, and skin. The sweat renders the thin, beige costumes see-through, so viewers notice not only the sweat and peat but also the bodies underneath. Thus, the audience becomes aware of the various shapes and sizes of the dancers' bodies. The peat, sweat, and visible chests and torsos draw attention to the individual bodies of the performers. These elements typically concealed in classical ballet call attention to the dancers' labor and fatigue. "The energy demanded from the dancers is not disguised, it confronts the audience directly," remarks choreographer Norbert Servos. "No smiles mask the strain, it is made audible by the dancers' heavy breathing" (Servos 1984, 30). Peat and sweat mark the dancers' skin, emphasizing the laborious nature of the choreography.

This raw, unapologetic presentation of bodies and perspiration prompted the disdain of dance critic Arlene Croce. In her review of *The Rite of Spring's* American premiere she proclaimed,

> By getting sweaty dancers dirty, the earth floor adds an element of yuck to "Sacre" which the other pieces don't have, but the dead leaves and the grass are bad enough: they made the Brooklyn Academy, which isn't air conditioned, smell like a stable. Naturally, you don't dance on such stages.
> (1984, 194)

The sweaty skin and dirty bodies created a "yuck" factor. Croce vividly describes the production as "sweating, heavy breathing, clammy bodies slapping against one another, peeling wet clothes from clammy bodies" (1984, 193). The *Oxford English Dictionary* defines "yuck" as an "expression of strong distaste or disgust," "messy, unpleasant, or distasteful material," and "the feeling of horror, revulsion, or disgust" (2022). The "dirty," "sweaty," "clammy" bodies in *The Rite of Spring* countered Croce's expectations that the dancers should conceal the efforts of their labor; sweat should not be visible and skin should appear smooth and blemish free. For Croce the performance evoked disgust. Disgust, according to law scholar William Ian Miller, "convey[s] a strong sense of aversion to something perceived as dangerous because of its powers to contaminate, infect, or pollute by proximity, contact or ingestion" (1997, 2). Feelings of disgust often signal that something may be potentially dangerous to the body. Neuroscientist Rachel Herz asserts that this is linked to acts that are not considered "civilized," or "polite" (2012, 43). Behaviors, such as "having sex, grunting, farting, belching, being naked, scratching ourselves … being unwashed, and squatting to urinate," are considered disgusting because "they do not uphold the conventions of civility that we expect and respect" (Herz 2012, 43). Humans are frequently repulsed by bodily functions because they are a reminder that we are, indeed, a part of the animal kingdom, and that the porosity of the human body makes it susceptible to contagions.

Croce's disdain of *The Rite of Spring's* "yuck" factor aligns with philosopher Julia Kristeva's assertion that abjection disturbs order. It is "not lack of cleanliness or health that causes abjection but what disturbs identity, system, order. What does not respect borders, positions, rules. The in-between, the ambiguous, the composite" (Kristeva 1982, 4). Peat is a composite of various chemicals and matter, as well as a liminal space that preserves bodies and prevents decomposition. Placed on stage in *The Rite of Spring*, it does not stay in one place. Its movement affects the dancers and audience. It disrupts expectations as it alters the smell and atmosphere of the venue, demonstrating that "natural" elements do not belong in "cultural" venues (at least according to Croce), as it renders them abject. Abjection is threatening to order because it jeopardizes systems by transgressing boundaries. As Kristeva argues,

> the sickly, acrid smell of sweat, of decay, does not *signify* death. No … refuse and corpses *show me* what I permanently thrust aside in order to live. These bodily fluids, this defilement … are what life withstands … There, I am at the border of my condition as a living being.
>
> (1982, 3, italics in original)

The liminal state of abjection reminds humans of their own mortality, while simultaneously emphasizing their state of being alive. Bodily fluids and stenches transgress constructed borders. Sweat and dirt highlight the permeability of the body.

Considering perspiration and peat through cultural theories of abjection reveals that skin and bodies are porous assemblages. Skin is not a neutral, unmarked surface (Ahmed and Stacey 2001), it is an organ affixed with regulations to impose order. Miller affirms that rules are placed on skin because it is considered dangerous and "it threatens or promises (depending on the context) the prospect of nakedness" (1997, 53). Clothing, or rather, the suppression of naked skin, within western/Anglo-Euro epistemologies, creates order because it allows the human body to be hierarchically categorized above animals and other organisms.[5] Peat, embedded into exposed skin and inhaled into nostrils, disrupts the anthropocentric hierarchy because it demonstrates that these categories are constructed.

Foregrounding peat, sweat, and bodies, *The Rite of Spring* challenges the audience to confront these "unpleasantries." Bausch does not impose classical ballet "regulations" on the dancers: she allows their "natural," "abject" states to emerge. Accentuating physical labor and bodily secretions, her choreography illuminates the constructions of what is considered "natural," and by extension what is considered "unnatural." The dancers' dirty, sweaty, exposed bodies create discomfort because they signal the materiality of bodies. As May asserts, ecocritical analysis of performance, "brings into focus the web of social, political, economic, and ecological systems that touch our bodies" (2007, 101). Croce's response demonstrates the ways in which the bodies in the performance (human and more-than-human) are enmeshed in extractive environmental logics. The economic systems and power structures that reduce peat to a resource are the same systems that inform spectators reading it as "dirty" in the context of performance. The peat renders the human bodies abject as it disrupts material boundaries and exhibits the limitations of anthropocentrism. Theorized through the scholarship of those working within relational frameworks, however, peat can be understood as more than just an abject substance.

Vital Peat

Sociology and education scholars Te Kawehau Hoskins (Ngati Hau) and Alison Jones (Pākehā) identify that, "in post-Enlightenment Western ontologies," ecological matter, like peat, is reduced to a resource and considered inanimate (2016, 80). Hoskins and Jones explain that in Maori and many other Indigenous ontologies, however, "'objects' – whether… a dead body, a forest or a piece of greenstone – [are] understood as determining events, as exerting forces, as volitional, or as instructing people, as speaking to us, and people [can] hear what they might tell" (2016, 80). This enables a reading of the peat as an active, animate performer that operates in relation to other bodies and forces.

Writing about "Place-Thought," an "understanding of the world via physical embodiment," within Haudenosaunee and Anishinaabe cosmologies, Indigenous studies scholar Vanessa Watts (Mohawk and Anishinaabe Bear Clan from Six Nations of the Grand River) explains that the "land is alive and thinking and that humans and non-humans derive agency through the extensions of these thoughts" (2013, 21). There is not a differentiation between place and thought, human and more-than-human; everything is interconnected. "The agency that place possesses can be thought of in a similar way that Western thinkers locate agency in human beings," expounds Watts (2013, 23). "If, as Indigenous peoples, we are extensions of the very land we walk upon, then we have an obligation to maintain communication with it" (Watts 2013, 23). Understood within "Place-Thought," land, beings, and thought are sentient and deeply embedded and embodied together. Building on the work of Watts and others,[6] geographer and sound artist Anja Kanngieser (non-Indigenous) and social anthropologist Zoe Todd's (Métis) "kin study" is a method that strives for "more embedded, expansive, material, and respectful relations to people and land" (2020, 385). They invite those studying environmental issues to "take seriously the relationality of the world and ourselves" (Kanngieser and Todd 2020, 389). Through Watts' "Place-Thought," and Kanngieser and Todd's "kin study," the peatbog can be understood as animate and profoundly embedded in its niche and broader environments. Its ecological processes sustain myriad lives as the bog absorbs carbon from the atmosphere, stores, and filters water and fosters diverse flora and fauna. If peat, within the context of a peatbog, is vital, sustaining itself and other lives, how can it be encountered in *The Rite of Spring* – where it has been displaced by humans and disconnected from its environment?

In some ways *The Rite of Spring* perhaps strives for an embeddedness of dancers/people and peat/place, as the choreography emphasizes the permeability of human bodies and ecological matter. But it is ultimately hampered by an overriding western framework as the peat was extracted from its habitat, stored in containers, spread on stage, and treated as a prop. There are no indications of its geographical origin, how it was obtained, or what became of it after the performance. There does not seem to be a consideration of the effects of the peat's removal or a comprehension of it beyond a resource. Kanngieser and Todd posit methods of "kin study" that attend to gaps in relationality such as those present in *The Rite of Spring*. To "[maintain] ethical and reciprocal relationships with Land and place" they propose "thinking through the local as much as the global implications of resource extraction," and conceiving of "place as kin rather than a substrate from which we take ideas" (Kanngieser and Todd 2020, 386, 391). While not practiced in *The Rite of Spring*, Kanngieser and Todd's approaches provide tangible methods for considering the ethics and multi-scalar effects of the peats use in the performance. The peat's extraction releases carbon into the atmosphere, which has local as well as global impacts. What local beings and ecological systems were affected or eradicated because of the peat's biogeocultography? If the peat had been treated as kin rather than resource, what might still be thriving locally and globally? Kanngieser and Todd's work illuminates the manifold ecological repercussions of the peat's presence in the performance, and the multitudinous perils of not maintaining embedded and materially specific relations with the land.

While the peat's displacement has multi-scalar effects, it does not strip it of its animacy. It retains its vitality and functions as a performer in the choreography by responding to the dancers' movements with its own "trajectories, propensities, [and] tendencies" (Bennett 2010, viii). The dancers' bodies must negotiate with it as they move through the space. Feminist philosopher

Nancy Tuana's conceptual metaphor of "viscous porosity," which attends to "sites of resistance and opposition [giving] attention to the complex ways in which material agency is often involved in interactions," is generative here (2008, 194). "Viscous porosity" concentrates on the ways that interactions among humans, more-than-humans, and other phenomena are not static or fluid, but often resistant, sticky, and complex. Applying this to the dancers and peat emphasizes that their relationship is permeable, but it also has sites of resistance. It is messy, literally and metaphorically. The peat's vitality in the performance is a reminder to the dancers and audience that it is not a passive inanimate object, even if it has been displaced and not treated as kin.[7]

The peat is both material performer and metaphor within the narrative. Metaphorically it represents the earth's soil and the ritual spilling of blood that must occur for the arrival of spring. Narratively, the physical presence of bodies in motion is jarring because it reminds the audience that one of these bodies will be terminated to complete the rite. The moving bodies on stage accentuate the fact that soon one body will be absent, eradicated to bring about spring. Materially, the peat is a more-than-human being on stage performing with the dancers. The "viscous porosity" of their relationship often makes the performance challenging. "The dancers have no need to act their growing exhaustion," confirms Servos, "it is genuine as they dance against the resistance of ankle-deep earth" (1984, 30). Traces of the dancers' movement are imprinted in the peat, an ephemeral physical record of the bodies' motion. The peat momentarily records the actions of the dancers until it is written over by other movement. The vitality of the displaced peat signifies a rupture among humans and more-than-humans (people and place), literally and metaphorically. This echoes Watts's assertion that colonization reduces land to dirt and only attributes agency to humans, estranging things that were never intended to be severed (2013, 32). Performance scholar Una Chaudhuri designates this schism as "zoögeopathology," "the infliction by humans, on [others]… the vicissitudes of displacement" (2012, 47). Partnering peat and humans in her choreography, Bausch stages a "zoögeopathologic" rupture in *The Rite of Spring*.

A close reading of the interactions among peat and dancers collapses notions of self and other and illuminates ecological relationality. As peat and humans dance together, their compositions change. Through "viscous porosity," the peat and dancers who began the piece are not the same who conclude it. As discussed in Chapter 1, performance studies scholar Dwight Conquergood argues that performance as movement can "transgress boundaries and trouble closure" (1995, 138). Even though the peat is displaced and not treated as kin, its animacy is apparent through the ways in which it unsettles anthropocentric boundaries, illuminating that "we are one species among many, among multitudes" (Chaudhuri 2012, 50). Through biogeocultography, the peat brings the materiality of the past into the present, troubling closure. These material remains are not passive; they assert their vitality as they perform.

Performative Taphonomy

In The *Rite of Spring*, the materiality of human and more-than-human bodies is made viscerally present in several ways. Narratively, one of the dancing bodies will be extinguished to complete the rite and return to the earth. This represents connections among the land and bodies, as bodies decompose, they become part of the soil ecosystem. However, bodies do not decompose in peat. They are preserved, creating an archeological archive. The peat used in *The Rite of Spring* contains organic remains of the past. Thus, the dancers perform a staged version of a rite in an element that conceivably contains human remains from ancient religious rituals (e.g., Lindow Man and other bog bodies). (Since the peats original habitat was not disclosed, we can only hypothesize about its contents.) Asserting its vitality, the peat responds to the dancers' movement by making their corporeality and bodily secretions visible. The "viscous porosity" among dancers/people and peat/place stages a "zoögeopathologic" rupture that exhibits the extractive logics of capitalism, which reduce peat to a resource, contribute to climate change, and erase history. Displacing peat not only releases carbon into the atmosphere but also destroys preserved bodies and objects. These artifacts, often eradicated before they are discovered, efface knowledge housed in the earth. As covered in Chapter 1, both taphonomy and historiography are concerned with the conditions that enable or hinder the presence of (ecological) materials through time. Systems of extractive capitalist logics impede preservation of material artifacts – expunging the past and its potential to be exhumed. However, the "zoögeopathologic" rupture staged in *The Rite of Spring* enacts a performative taphonomy. The peat's biogeocultography transports ecologically situated remains into the present. Placed on stage, the peat and the particulates of the past that comprise it, assert their vitality by performing and marking the bodies of the human dancers. Boundaries are reterritorialized as humans, peat, and material remains merge, creating "viscously porous," relations. The dancers' bodies altered through these interactions now carry the peat and material remains with them. In this way the organic matter erased through the peat's disinterment exists in perpetuity within the dancer's reterritorialized bodies.

Analyzing the relations among peat and dancers in *The Rite of Spring* indicates larger ruptures among people and place, political and economic systems. The extracted peat exhibits the limitations of anthropocentric worldviews. Exploring unexpected intersections of power structures and ecological matter, anthropologist Anna Lowenhaupt Tsing states,

> global landscapes today are strewn with… ruin. Still, these places can be lively despite announcements of their death; abandoned asset fields sometimes yield new multispecies and multicultural life.
>
> (2015, 6)

As Tsing deftly illuminates, places of decay, like peatbogs, yield multispecies life, offering opportunities to reconsider human and more-than-human relations. Humans, in anthropocentric ontologies, need to become more connected with multispecies life. *The Rite of Spring*, through the peat's biogeocultography, exposes a multiplicity of ecological matter, which deserve attunement.

In Chapter 3, I delve deeper into the dirt, to explore the organisms within it. Focusing on dirt in Eveoke Dance Theatre's *Las Mariposas*, I argue that through the affective relationships among the organisms that reside in the dirt and on the dancers' skin, the dancers *become*-dirt and the dirt *becomes*-human. Using performance and ecocritical theory, this chapter argues that these relationships disrupt anthropocentrism by revealing the presence of other invisible materials in the interaction (protozoa, bacteria, lipids, etc.). Dancer and dirt choreography in *Las Mariposas* demonstrate that the performer is not always human.

Notes

1 As the piece progresses, viewers realize that the red cloth is the dress that the Chosen One wears for her final dance.
2 There is much written about *The Rite of Spring's* choreography and music. I only detail the aspects of the production history that are relevant to my argument.
3 Bausch's training began in 1955, at the Folkwang School in Germany, under director Kurt Jooss. Jooss trained under Rudolf Laban and Mary Wigman, two significant figures of European Modern dance.
4 This is not the first-time ecology has been put in conversation with Bausch's *The Rite of Spring*. In their article, "Matter, Life, Sex, and Death: Ecosexuality and Pina Bausch's *Rite of Spring*," Michael J. Morris (2018) uses an ecosexual framework to analyze the production.
5 I want to note that agency has not been universally attributed to all humans. There have been many humans, past and present, who have been categorized by colonial and settler colonial systems of power as inhuman and inanimate. As Kim TallBear (Sisseton-Wahpeton Oyate), drawing on the work of Mel Chen, writes, "the animacy hierarchy also de-animates many humans, including Indigenous and Black people, by placing them below the Western and often male subject" (2019, 25). Additionally, Kathryn Yusoff, discussing the white geology of the Anthropocene, affirms "geology is a racial formation built on the labor of Black and Indigenous peoples who were categorized, by white, colonial systems of power, as inhuman matter" (2018, 6).
6 Kanngieser and Todd's "kin study" also draws on the work of Mohawk scholar Sandra Styres. Styres, Sandra. 2019. "Literacies of the Land: Decolonizing Narratives, Storying, and Literature." In *Indigenizing and Decolonizing Studies in Education: Mappin the Long View*, edited Linda Tuhiwai Smith, Eve Tuck, and K. Wayne Yang, 24–73. New York: Routledge.
7 While peat is indeed a performer, I do not mean to suggest that power is equally distributed or fixed as it has not been treated ethically or relationally.

References

Ahmed, Sara, and Jackie Stacey. 2001. "Introduction: Dermographies." In *Thinking through the Skin*, edited by Sara Ahmed and Jackie Stacey, 15–32. New York: Routledge.

Bausch, Pina. December 3, 1975. *Le Sacre Du Printemps*. Opernhaus Wuppertal, Wuppertal, Germany.

Béjart, Maurice. December 8, 1959. *Le Sacre Du Printemps*. Théâtre Royal de la Monnaie, Brussels, Belgium.

Bennett, Jane. 2010. *Vibrant Matter*. Durham: Duke University Press.

Browne, Malcolm W. 1988. "'Bog Man' Reveals Story of a Brutal Ritual." *New York Times*. Accessed July 20, 2021. https://www.nytimes.com/1988/01/26/science/bog-man-reveals-story-of-a-brutal-ritual.html.

Cass, Joan. 1993. *Dancing through History*. New Jersey: Prentice Hall.

Chaudhuri, Una. 2012. "The Silence of the Polar Bears: Performing (Climate) Change in the Theatre of Species." In *Readings in Performance and Ecology*, edited by Wendy Arons and Theresa J. May, 45–58. New York: Palgrave Macmillan.

Cody, Gabrielle. 1998. "Woman, Man, Dog, Tree: Two Decades of Intimate and Monumental Bodies in Pina Bausch's Tanztheater." *The Drama Review* 42, no. 2: 115–132.

Conquergood, Dwight. 1995. "Of Caravans and Carnivals: Performance Studies in Motion." *Drama Review* 39, no. 4: 137–141.

Croce, Arlene. 1984. "Bausch's Theatre of Dejection." In *The Pina Bausch Sourcebook: The Making of Tanztheater*, edited by Royd Climenhaga, 192–195. New York: Routledge.

Curtis, John T. 1959. *The Vegetation of Wisconsin*. Madison: The University of Wisconsin Press.

Fischer-Lichte, Erika. 2005. *Theatre, Sacrifice, Ritual: Exploring Forms of Political Theatre*. New York: Routledge.

Gewin, Virginia. 2020. "How Peat Could Protect the Planet." *Nature* 578: 2-4-208. Accessed August 13, 2021. https://www.nature.com/articles/d41586-020-00355-3.

Graham, Martha. 1984. *Le Sacre Du Printemps*. New York State Theatre, New York, New York.

Hancock, Mark H., Daniela Klein, Roxane Andersen, and Neil R. Cowie. 2018. "Vegetation Response to Restoration Management of a Blanket Bog Damaged by Drainage and Afforestation." *Applied Vegetation Science* 21, no. 2: 167–178.

Herz, Rachel. 2012. *That's Disgusting: Unraveling the Mysteries of Repulsion*. New York: W. W. Norton & Company.

Jones, Alison, and Te Kawehau Hoskins. 2016. "A Mark on Paper: The Matter of Indigenous-Settler History." In *Posthuman Research Practices in Education*, 75–92. London: Palgrave.

Kanngieser, Anja, and Zoe Todd. 2020. "From Environmental Case Study to Environmental Kin Study." *History and Theory* 59, no. 3: 385–393.

Kristeva, Julia. 1982. *Powers of Horror*. Translated by Louis-Ferdinand Celine. New York: Columbia University Press.

Liping, Yang. 2018. *The Rite of Spring*. Shanghai International Art Festival, Shanghai, China.

Lobell, Jarrett A. and Samir S. Patel. 2010a. "Bog Bodies Rediscovered." *Archaeology* 63, no. 3. Accessed July 19, 2022. https://archive.archaeology.org/1005/bogbodies/.

Lobell, Jarrett A. and Samir S. Patel. 2010b. "Bog Science." *Archaeology* 63, no. 3. Accessed July 19, 2022. https://archive.archaeology.org/1005/bogbodies/bog_science.html.

Loney, Glenn. 1985. "'I Pick My Dancers as People': Pina Bausch Discusses Her Work with the Wuppertal Dance Theatre." In *The Pina Bausch Sourcebook*, edited by Royd Climenhaga, 88–98. New York: Routledge.

Massine, Léonide. 1920. *Le Sacre Du Printemps.*. Théâtre Champs-Elysées, Paris, France.
May, Theresa J. May. 2007. "Beyond Bambi: Toward a dangerous ecocriticism in theatre studies." *Theatre Topics* 17, no. 2: 95–110.
Miller, William Ian. 1997. *The Anatomy of Disgust.* Cambridge: Harvard University Press.
Morris, Michael J. 2018. "Matter, Life, Sex, and Death: Ecosexuality and Pina Bausch's *The Rite of Spring.*" *Dance Chronicle* 41, no. 3: 335–358.
"Peat." n.d. *International Peat Society.* Accessed August 13, 2021. https://peatlands.org/peat/.
"Peatlands and Climate Change." n.d. *International Union for Conservation of Nature.* Accessed August 13, 2021. https://www.iucn.org/resources/issues-briefs/peatlands-and-climate-change.
Riding, Alan. 1997. "Using Muscles Classical Ballet Has No Need For." *The New York Times*, June 15, 1997. Accessed July 19, 2022. https://www.nytimes.com/1997/06/15/arts/using-muscles-classical-ballet-has-no-need-for.html.
Servos, Norbert, and Gert Weigelt. 1984. *Pina Bausch – Wuppertal Dance Theater Or the Art of Training a Goldfish: Excursions into Dance.* Translated from the German by Patricia Stadié, 30. Ballett-Bühnen Verlag.
TallBear, Kim. 2019. "Caretaking Relations, not American Dreaming." *Kalfou* 6, no. 1: 24–41.
Tsing, Anna Lowenhaupt. 2015. *The Mushroom at the End of the World.* Princeton: Princeton University Press.
Tuana, Nancy. 2008. "Viscous Porosity: Witnessing Katrina." In *Material Feminisms*, edited by Stacy Alaimo and Susan Hekman, 188–213. Bloomington: Indiana University Press.
Williams, Faynia. 1997. "Working with Pina Bausch: A Conversation with Tanztheater Wuppertal." *TheatreForum* Issue 10: 74.
"What is the Global Peatlands Initiative?" 2016. *Global Peatlands Initiative.* Accessed August 13, 2021. https://www.globalpeatlands.org/.
Watts, Vanessa. 2013. "Indigenous Place-Thought and Agency amongst Humans and Non-humans (First Woman and Sky Woman go on a European world tour!)." *Decolonization: Indigeneity, Education & Society* 2, no. 1: 20–34.
Wigman, Mary. 1957. *Le Sacre Du Printemps.* Städtische Oper Berlin, Berlin, Germany.
Wim, Wenders, director. *Pina.* 2011. IFC Films Unlimited, 1 hr., 43 min.
"Yuck." *Oxford English Dictionary.* 2022. Accessed July 19, 2022. https://www.oed.com/view/Entry/232526?rskey=cXS6dB&result=3#eid.
Yusoff, Kathryn. 2018. *A Billion Black Anthropocenes or None.* Minneapolis: University of Minnesota Press.

3 A Dirty *Pas De Deux*

Dirt, Skin, and "Trans-corporeality" in Eveoke Dance Theatre's *Las Mariposas*

A dancer wearing a bright purple dress stands ankle-deep in a tall bin of dirt. She touches her chest, then her face. She commences a *port-de-bras*, arms out, up, and around as she slowly walks through the dirt, and then extends her leg into an *arabesque*. Suddenly, she begins to convulse, expanding and contracting her torso. A second dancer, dressed in a brown shirt and pants, rolls upstage of the bin. She begins digging dirt out of the bin with her bare hands, sending large handfuls flying through the air. The digging becomes more frantic as she uses her entire body to dislodge the dirt. Eventually, the second dancer climbs into the bin and begins a tightly choreographed struggle with the dancer in purple, dominating her, as dirt covers their bodies, propels through the air, and coats the stage floor. Dirt continues to fly as the dancer in purple thrashes to resist the turbulent motion of the dancer in brown. Finally, the dancer in purple ceases to move, her energy extinguished by the violent control of the second dancer. In this exchange from Eveoke Dance Theatre's *Las Mariposas* (2010), dirt much like peat in The *Rite of Spring* is a dynamic performer in the choreography.[1]

This chapter concentrates on Eveoke Dance Theatre's *Las Mariposas*, which was adapted for the stage from Julia Alvarez's novel *In the Time of the Butterflies* (1994) and performed in the United States (2010) and the Dominican Republic (2011). In *Las Mariposas*, dancers and dirt partner not only with one another in a *pas de deux* but also with the myriad more-than-human beings that reside in the dirt and on dancers' bodies, creating an ecologically complex *pas de millions,* so to speak. Pairing dancer interviews with Gilles Deleuze and Félix Guattari's theories of *becoming* (1987), I explore the ways in which the physical interactions among the dancers and dirt enabled them to form affective relationships that restructured their material composition. Using posthuman (Braidotti 2006; Alaimo 2008) and performance theories (Taylor 2003; Woynarski 2020), I contend that these affective relationships disrupt anthropocentric conceptions of humanity by revealing the presence of other invisible ecological matter (protozoa, bacteria, lipids etc.), demonstrating that the performer is not always human. This close reading of *Las Mariposas* maintains that humans – in performance and everyday life – are

DOI: 10.4324/9781003164234-4

A Dirty Pas De Deux 59

not discretely bounded, but permeable and dynamic. This chapter concludes by questioning how "trans-corporeality" (Alaimo 2008) might alter performance paradigms. There is a robust body of scholarship exploring Latin American ecofeminism, ecocriticism, and ecologies, including work by Sarah D. Wald et al. (2019), Macarena Gómez-Barris (2017), Adrian Taylor Kane (2014), José Manuel Marrero Henríquez (2019), Mary Judith Ress (2006), and Laura Barbas-Rhoden (2019), to name a few. While these scholars explore the intersections of people and place in Latin America and Latino/a/x cultures, most of them focus on cultural texts and literature, rather than the performing arts. In this chapter, I place dance and performance studies, in conversation with ecocriticism to examine the entanglements of movement, performance, and materiality in *Las Mariposas*.

Las Mariposas and Dirt

In 2010, Eveoke Dance Theatre,[2] a non-profit dance company and school located in San Diego, California, created *Las Mariposas,* an imaginative adaptation of Alvarez's novel, which tells the story of the Mirabal sisters, who led an underground resistance – known as the Fourteenth of June Movement – in the 1950s, against Dominican dictator Rafael Leonidas Trujillo. Through dance and recorded narration, *Las Mariposas* presents the story of Dedé, Minerva, María Teresa, and Patria Mirabal. It creatively embodies moments spanning their entire lives: from their childhood years on a farm; to learning about the violence of Trullijo's regime as young adults and converting their childhood home into a place of resistance; to their time spent in prison; and finally, to three of sisters' deaths at the hands of Trujillo's soldiers.[3] Young adult dancers portray adolescent versions of Dedé (who was not murdered), Minerva, María Teresa, and Patria Mirabal, and adult dancers portray older versions of the sisters.[4] Five other dancers represent various characters throughout the course of the piece. *Las Mariposas* premiered in 2010 at the 10th Avenue Theatre in San Diego, California. Alvarez saw a studio rehearsal of the production and told the cast and crew that they needed to take *Las Mariposas* to the Dominican Republic (Spalink and Whitlock 2012). Her suggestion planted the idea for a Dominican tour, and in 2011, Eveoke performed *Las Mariposas* at the Gran Teatro del Cibao in Santiago, at the Mauricio Baez Centro Cultural in Santo Domingo, and in Villa Tapia as part of the festival Hermanas Mirabal.[5] Evangeline Rose Whitlock, the production's stage manager, and I did a presentation on the production, and its use of dirt, at the Earth Matters on Stage conference in Pittsburgh, Pennsylvania (2012). Whitlock had been on tour with the company, and in our presentation, we integrated her hands-on experiences, interviews with the company, and my ecocritical research to explore the numerous implications of incorporating dirt into performance.

During the Dominican Republic tour, the production was staged in three different venues, with playing spaces ranging from 32 by 40 feet to 24 by 32 feet. During each performance, a large wooden altar was located upstage center and three bins, each 5 by 2 by 3 feet and filled to the brim with dirt, stood around the altar, two on stage left and one on stage right. Another dirt bin of the same size was located downstage right. Over the course of the two-hour production, the dancers rolled in, kicked, held, threw, and dug the dirt, causing it to disperse over the entire playing space and collect on their bodies. Artistic Director Erika Malone and choreographer Ericka Aisha Moore incorporated dirt into the production because the Mirabal sisters' garden and farm, and the Dominican landscape, were so prominent in Alvarez's book. The landscape of the Dominican Republic is crucial to all of Alvarez's writing, asserts literature scholar Kelli Lyon Johnson (2005, 5). Literature scholars Rebecca L. Harrison and Emily Hipchen confirm that Alvarez's work is invested in "preserving… respect for the land, the animals, and the people who provide sustenance" (2013, 18). For Moore, the use of dirt felt pivotal to Eveoke's adaptation. She stated,

> For me… dirt … was like the life force. The life-force of the family, of the community… because how we treat our dirt is how we cultivate ourselves. So if we treat our dirt badly, then what's coming out of that is not gonna be that positive. But if we nurture our dirt what comes out of that I think would be so great.
>
> (2012)

The dirt was not only integral to the performance, but gathering and restoring it every night became a significant part of the post-show process for the cast. After each performance of *Las Mariposas*, the dancers would return to stage to sweep and collect the dirt, returning it to the bins for the next performance. For some, this act became a post-show ritual, and the performance did not feel complete until the dirt had been restored to the bins. Once the run of the show ended, the dirt was returned to the places from which it was borrowed.[6]

It is perhaps helpful to pause here to describe one of the key scenes (see Figure 3.1). The murder of the Mirabal sisters is one of the most memorable and haunting scenes in *Las Mariposas*. The choreography is violent, frantic, and unapologetic; it was danced with unbridled energy, agility, strength, and specificity. The dancers playing the sisters each stand in their own bin of dirt and slowly walk through it. They gracefully extend their arms toward one another and then back to themselves as they grope their own bodies and grasp at the air. The tension is apparent in their arms as they appear to search for an anchor. The sisters finally reach down and touch the dirt and for a brief moment appear to find grounding in this connection. But the moment is short-lived, as the sisters' bodies begin expanding, contracting, convulsing, and writhing

Figure 3.1 (From left to right) Nikki Dunnan as Dedé Mirabal, ensemble dancers Becky Hurt, Molly Terbovich-Ridenhour, Bruce Walker, and Shayna Cribbs, and Charlene Penner as the Butterfly in the scene "Unearthing the Girls" from the performance at the Gran Teatro del Cibao in Santiago, Dominican Republic, Tuesday, November 29, 2011. Photo by Tim Botsko.

into the dirt. While the sisters are dancing in their bins, the ensemble dancers portraying the murderers scuttle onto stage, moving on all fours as one unit. They break apart into individual dancers but remain in full frontal contact with the floor before each emerges onto all fours and slinks toward the bins in which the sisters are dancing. Once the ensemble dancers reach the bins, they use their arms and legs to embrace the bins and tumble around them. Then the ensemble dancers reach into the bins and begin throwing out handfuls of dirt; thus commences the choreography of the murder. The ensemble dancers dig enough dirt out of the bins to allow the sisters to fit within them; fingers, hands, and torsos collide with the dirt as it is displaced from the bins onto the stage. Once there is room for bodies in the bins, each of the ensemble dancers grabs a sister and forces her down into the dirt that remains in the bin. The choreography of the killing yields a violent and grotesquely beautiful performance of stylized, articulated, distraught movement embodying domination and resistance, brutal assault, and the will to survive, all while dirt – and the microbes, fungi, and protozoa contained within it – spews into the air, colliding with the bodies and faces of the dancers. The sisters vocalize the struggle through screams and grunts. The thrashing movement between the sisters and the murderers gradually becomes slower and less vigorous until finally the movement comes to a complete halt. This moment of stillness is a jarring and

Figure 3.2 In "The Cemetery is Beginning to Flower," (the scene following the murder) dirt coats the stage and many of the dancers. Photo by Tim Botsko.

poignant juxtaposition to their earlier frantic violence. The "life force" of the three Mirabal sisters has been extinguished, and the bins of dirt transform into the graves in which they are buried. Piles of dirt coat the stage. The ensemble dancers slowly back off the stage, minute particles of dirt and other ecological matter clinging to their skin, creating a microcosm of interspecies relations. As they shrink away from the scene, they leave traces and imprints in the dirt (see Figure 3.2).

Becoming Dirt, *Becoming* Human

As discussed in the book's introduction, dirt comprises abiotic and biotic elements such as sand, silt, clay, minerals, fungi, plants, and bacteria; species from all biological kingdoms live in the soil (Nardi 2007). "Organisms *are* soil," elucidates feminist philosopher María Puig de la Bellacasa (2017 189, italics in original). "A lively soil can only exist with and through a multispecies community of biota that *makes* it, that contributes to is creation" (Bellacasa 2017, 189, italics in original). Soil is not solely decomposed material, or habitat, but rather a living web. Soil's organismal web is subject to the same pressures as any ecosystem, competing for resources and struggling for survival. Many of these organisms occupy niches that are involved in the decay of organic matter such as dead plants and animals, from which they acquire the resources necessary for survival and in turn release vital nutrients back into the soil. In this way, soil turns death into a vital source of life as nutrients are released.

In each production of *Las Mariposas*, the dirt was locally sourced. The San Diego productions featured Sand Diego dirt, while the Dominican Republic tour used dirt from Santiago, Santo Domingo, and Villa Tapia. The dirt, comprised of geographically specific abiotic and biotic elements, exhibited an environmental history of local plants, animals, and microscopic organisms. The dirt's organismal web becomes entangled with the dancers, affecting them and their performances. Deleuze and Guattari describe affect as something that changes or *becomes* when two bodies (or more) encounter one another. In a group interview conducted by Whitlock with ensemble members Bruce Walker, Becky Hurt, Molly Terbovich-Ridenhour, and Shayna Cribbs, the dancers articulated that when they rehearsed and performed the murder scene, they felt that they lost a sense of self and became something else (2012). Cribbs describes the experience:

> I feel like with the soil, I felt this like, energy in it, as I was digging it. And I don't know if it was because of the physical exertion, that was creating this energy between me and the soil and I could just feel it at my fingertips as I was digging. And then the energy just was like, almost like this whirlwind and getting bigger and bigger and bigger. And some nights, I ... lost all sense of self. I had no idea who I was. I wasn't a person; I was just like all arms and dirt and flinging and energy and... I was not me.
>
> (2012)

Hurt describes her experience in similarly compelling terms:

> I actually appreciated the physical exertion that had to happen for us to get all the dirt out [of the bins]. And there was a goal, like we had to get a certain amount of dirt [out] before the [dancers portraying the sisters] would fall [into the bins], before we could actually do the choreography of killing them. And you are fucking tired and you have to keep going, and literally like-taking their life source, 'cause soil is so representative of life, and also it's so eerie-like we're digging their graves almost! And so there was that physical like, oh your legs are in the way, fuck, you know, just completely out of-not out of body-but you just lose a sense of self when you are that physical. You lose a sense of like, reason, or why you're doing it.
>
> (2012)

The ensemble dancers contended that it was their relationship with the dirt that allowed them to perform the choreography of the murder. Affect theory allows an exploration of the possible ways that the dancers' physical interactions with the dirt allowed them to *become* something other than themselves.

Deleuze and Guattari develop their theory of affect, what they term *becoming*, in *A Thousand Plateaus*, where they state,

> To every relation of movement and rest, speed and slowness grouping together infinity of parts, there corresponds a degree of power. To the relations composing, decomposing, or modifying an individual there correspond intensities that affect it, augmenting or diminishing its power to act; these intensities come from external parts or from the individual's own parts. Affects are becomings... Becoming is to emit particles that take on certain relations of movement and rest because they enter a particular zone of proximity. Or, it is to emit particles that enter that zone because they take on those relations.
>
> (1987, 256, 273)

Matter moving at various speeds exchange particles with other matter in its proximity, decomposing their initial boundaries and restructuring their material composition. This continuous transmission creates the conditions for an affective exchange between the bodies. In *Las Mariposas,* the choreography generated an exchange between particles in the dirt and those on the dancers. Many of the dancers stated that they felt they *became* something else while dancing with the dirt; in effect, the dirt augmented their power to act. For example, Cribbs said that digging the dirt made her feel more "animalistic," while Walker observed that the frenetic movement of digging the dirt in the death scene made him feel as if he had become a "murderer" (2012). The dancers' characterization of feeling "animalistic" and like a "murderer" seems to position the dirt as less than human. Their altered embodiment indicates that work with the dirt reduced them to something non-human, which for some had negative connotations. This perception of the dirt demonstrates the limitations of interspecies performance created within a western dualistic framework.

Even though each described it in slightly different terms, the ensemble dancers all agreed that during the murder scene, they felt as though they lost a sense of self when their bodies connected and collided with the dirt. Deleuze and Guattari assert that we know nothing of a body until we can comprehend how it is affected by or affects other bodies. When a body affects another body, they *become* different entities. For the ensemble dancers, it seems that their interactions with the dirt affected their bodies in a manner that caused them to lose a personal sense of self and enhanced their capacity to perform the choreography of the murder.

When the murder scene was blocked, the ensemble dancers initially had a difficult time partnering with the dirt. Working with the dirt presented considerable challenges, specifically for Terbovich-Ridenhour, who declared, "I think [it] physically made me sick for two months. And so I hated the dirt. I hated breathing the dirt, I hated the smell of it" (2012). For Hurt, the most difficult moment with the dirt was "the dance after the death scene where the dirt is everywhere. We get dirty. It was awful" (2012). The ensemble dancers concluded that working with this element did not feel natural; it felt "dirty" and uncomfortable and most of them confessed that initially they hated working with it. The dancers' aversion to the dirt aligns with feminist philosopher Julia Kristeva's argument – as discussed in Chapter 2 – that abjection disturbs systems because it transgresses boundaries and regulations (1982). "Dirt offends against order," contends anthropologist Mary Douglas (1966, 2–3). "Eliminating it is not a negative movement, but a positive effort to organize the environment" (Douglas 1966, 2–3). Within a western nature/culture binary, dirt is typically perceived as something "outside," in "nature." Here, it was brought into the theatre, conventionally conceived of as a cultural space (e.g., Croce's 1984 review of *The Rite of Spring* in Chapter 2) and used as a production element. The dirt permeated the dancers' bodies and created debris in the theatre, transgressing constructed boundaries.

The dancers' initial aversion to the dirt eventually began to shift as Moore, the choreographer, encouraged them to perceive the dirt as an extension of the body, rather than something offensive to it, stating:

> The body is not always enough to convey all the things that I want to convey. Because sometimes you just can't throw a body the way you can throw dirt. The way dirt moves through fingers. Through hands. Your body doesn't move that way. The dirt is an extension of the body. An extension of the experience.
>
> (2012)

As the dancers continued working with the dirt, their perceptions of it changed, allowing for a deterritorialization (a disruption of existing boundaries/relationships), and reterritorialization (a restructuring of those boundaries). The relationship that occurred among dancers and dirt emulates Deleuze's description of the fluid, intangible affect that flows through an orchid and wasp during pollination; "the two [becoming-wasp of the orchid and a becoming-orchid of the wasp] becomings interlink and form relays in the circulation of intensities pushing the deterritorialization even further" (1993, 3). Dancers and dirt exchanged particles and organisms, disrupting/ deterritorializing their initial material compositions and restructuring/reterritorializing them. Through their interactions, the dancers and dirt were both materially altered. The conventional constructed relationship between them was disrupted and an affective relationship formed, resulting in the dancers being unable to tell where body ended, and dirt began. As Cribbs described it earlier, her relationship with the dirt in the murder scene made her feel as though she lost a sense of self. Here, as with Deleuze's wasp and orchid, the deterritorialization and reterritorialization occurs, only instead of two entities, there might be thousands upon thousands of organisms in the relationship.

The dancers agreed that their perceived loss of self and *becoming* other was distinctly connected with their corporeal relationship with the dirt, as each noted that their bodies were in some way altered. The physical engagement with the dirt shifted their perception of it from an abject object to an entity on stage with which they had to perform. The application of affect theory to the dancer-dirt relationship illuminates that through their interaction with the dirt, the dancers *became* dirt. If the dancers did *become* dirt, is it possible that in return the dirt began to *become* human?

Discussing the complex affects that circulate through human and more-than-human worlds, ecofeminist scholar Stacy Alaimo posits that skin has the power to "[dissolve] a distinctly human identity," because of its liminality and "its intimacy with the 'outside' world" (1998, 134). Skin is a permeable membrane that connects with other bodies. It is also "an ecosystem, harboring microbial communities that live in a range of physiologically and topographically distinct niches," according to dermatologist Elizabeth A. Grice (Grice et al. 2009, 1190). When skin and dirt touch, molecular and interspecies interactions occur; cells, bacteria, lipids, and water leave the skin and enter the dirt. The dirt and skin affect one another, creating an ecologically intricate exchange. For Alaimo, skin functions similarly to Deleuze's rhizome, as skin is "a threshold where nature and culture dissolve, a rhizomatic place that connects 'desperate distances' through elemental relations" (1998, 137). Skin is an interface, a conduit between human and more-than-human beings. From its liminal position – as an exterior membrane and interior vessel for muscles, bones, and organs – skin crosses boundaries and dissolves anthropocentric hierarchies through horizontal enmeshment. The liminality of skin aids in the process of *becoming;* its permeability affects exchanges among bodies and ecological matter. Analyzing *Las Mariposas* through Alaimo's theories bolster the notion that the dancers *became* dirt, and that the dirt subsequently *became* human (see Figure 3.3). The dirt alters the dancers' physical composition and movement by seeping into their pores, clogging their nostrils, and impairing their eyesight. The dirt distributes cells, bacteria, and protozoa on the dancers, while the dancers deposit water, salts, oils, bacteria, hairs, and skin cells into the dirt. Both are transformed. Next, I explore the dynamics of these affective relationships.

"Transpositions" and "Bioperformativity"

Affect enables bodies to be open to experiencing other bodies. As dancers and dirt interact, their compositions are altered, but what are the dynamics of these relations? In this section, I use posthuman and performance theories to examine the ways in which these relationships stretch the capacity of the human body, exhibit the (bio)performativity of the dirt, and unsettle anthropocentric constructs of bodily discreteness.

Figure 3.3 Nikki Dunnan as Dedé Mirabal dancing in a bin of dirt. From the performance at the Centro Cultural Mauricio Baez in Santo Domingo, Dominican Republic, Thursday December 1, 2011. Photo by Tim Botsko.

"Trans-corporeality," for Alaimo, is "the time-space where human corporeality, in all its material fleshiness, is inseparable from 'nature' or 'environment'" (2008, 238). The human body does not function in isolation; it is a complex ecosystem in constant interplay with other ecosystems, the discrete limits of which are indefinable. Building from a trans-corporeal foundation, feminist philosopher Rosi Braidotti proffers a posthuman philosophy of transposing difference and *becoming* other. Her philosophy of "transpositions" "[explore] the possibility of a system of ethical values that ... rests on a nonunitary, nomadic, or rhizomatic view" (2006, 5). This ethic is not heterogenic or centered on the human body. It values all living organisms and is "based on... interconnections" (2006, 5). "Transpositions" are an ethics of *becoming,* of exchanges between species and bodies, of relationships in flux.

Engaging in transpositional ethics requires working toward the eradication of anthropocentrism, which, for Braidotti, is critical to create interspecies community. She posits "becoming animal" as one method to disrupt anthropocentrism, which has "nothing to do with metaphor of animality ... It is rather a case that requires a shift of the ontological ground of embodiment" (2006, 102). "Becoming-animal" is an embodied modification. It requires humans to forsake occularcentrism and attempt to perceive the world through various senses, as animals do. Discussing the sensorial experiences of animals, anthropologist Barbara Noske states,

> Not many people have seriously tried to imagine what it must be like to perceive and conceive the world in terms of "olfactory images" (such as dogs must do) ... or "acoustic pictures" (as dolphins and whales must do) ... humans are heavily biased towards the visual... seeing is believing... but for a dog scenting is believing.
>
> (1989, 158)

This is perhaps an oversimplification, as all animals perceive the world through a multitude of stimuli; and it does not acknowledge that not all humans perceive the world primarily through sight. It is, interesting, however, for those who rely on sight to consider the implications of depending upon other senses. For Braidotti, "A nomadic post-anthropocentric philosophy displaces the primacy of the visual... [and] is connected to an expansion or creation of new sensorial and perceptive capacities or powers, which alter or stretch what a body can actually do" (2006, 103). To *become* other, humans must push their bodies to perceive with multiple senses, perhaps stretching them past traditional limits, deterritorializing conventional functions, and reterritorializing them into something different.

In *Las Mariposas,* it is the very relationship between dancers and dirt that displaces the visual and allows the dancers to *become* other. The dancers recall how the dirt affected their vision. Cribbs describes how the dirt irritated her eyes and made it difficult to see (2012). Similarly, Walker recalls dirt infiltrating his eyes, even though they were closed while he was submerged in the dirt (2012). The dancers could smell it and feel it against their bodies; they experienced it through multiple senses and it in turn affected their movement. They danced with dirt in and on their bodies, and they dug it out of the bins until they were physically exhausted. Their olfactory, tactile, and kinesthetic interactions with the dirt pushed their bodies to the conventional limits of what a dancing body can perform, much like Braidotti's post-anthropocentric philosophy.

Braidotti's philosophy also requires recognition of the inherent vitality of the dirt and its organismal web. Much like the peat in *The Rite of Spring*, the dirt in *Las Mariposas*, was not passive but rather asserted its vitality in ways that were sometimes painful and difficult, but ultimately transformative for the dancers. Performance scholar Lisa Woynarski's concept of "bioperformativity," "the biological/material and the performative effects of things," further demonstrates the dirt's capabilities to perform (2020, 71). Woynarski carefully clarifies that this is "not to suggest that these things perform in the same way but to acknowledge their performativity and capacity to create effects, in different contexts, in different degrees and kinds" (2020, 72). Considering the dirt's vitality through "bioperformativity" exhibits how it performs, through its movement and affects. For instance, even though the choreography in *Las Mariposas* remained the same in each performance, the way the dirt performed with the dancers differed; that is, its dispersion and collision with various parts of the dancers' bodies were unique in each performance. "And so the struggle with the dirt… it is so unpredictable," notes Moore; "You kick it one way and now it's in this person's face and they're dancing with one eye closed because the dirt is in their eye" (2012). The composition of the dirt itself varied across performances. There were several different batches of dirt used for the California performances, and the Dominican Republic performances used dirt from each tour location. The dancers discussed how one batch was full of tiny rocks that made it painful to dance, while another one contained manure with an overpowering smell (Walker and Hurt 2012). The dirt not only traveled in unpredictable patterns but also interacted with the dancers' bodies in unique ways based on its composition. "Bioperformativity" evinces the dirt as another performer on stage.

The "bioperformativity" of the dirt also operated narratively within *Las Mariposas*. For Malone, the Artistic Director, and Moore, the choreographer, the dirt was crucial for both the choreography (the specific motion of the dirt) and the narrative (it grounded the story in a specific place and geography). Latin American literature scholar Adrian Taylor Kane confirms the importance of the "imagery of the natural world" in Latin American literature (2014, 1). That nature, in various ways, "has remained embedded in cultural discourses and historical projects throughout the centuries in Latin America" (Kane 2014, 1). Latin American environmental humanities scholar Laura Barbas-Rhoden contends that because landscape is so prominent in

"Latin American cultural texts," intersectional ecocritical inquiries are critical (2019, 1). She asserts that

> Reading Latin American cultural texts ecocritically... [requires] a constant grappling with... the dynamism of sociocultural realities, as these are shaped by human actions (for example, political events) and material forces (like volcanic eruptions), and their interplay (epidemic disease, natural disasters).
>
> (Barbas-Rhoden 2019, 71–72)

The geographic specificity of the Dominican landscape is crucial to the narrative of *Las Mariposas*. But as Barbas-Rhoden maintains, an ecocritical reading of the performance requires intersecting the social, material, and biological. The local dirt used during the performances in the Dominican Republic potentially contained remains that were present during Trujillo's regime. The dirt that (possibly) bore witness to those histories is now being used to tell one (of the many) stories of the people affected by the state violence.

Performance studies scholar Diana Taylor establishes a link between the representational practices of performance and science. She designates this as "the DNA of performance" and uses it to consider the "genetic and performatic" aspects of the Abuelas and Madres de Plaza de Mayo protests, which condemn the human rights atrocities committed during Argentina's Dirty War, especially the disappearance of children (Taylor 2003, 171, 175). Taylor describes how "the Abuelas and Madres performed the evidence [i.e., DNA, clothes, pictures, etc.,] by placing it on their bodies as they took to the Plaza" (2003, 173). Taylor argues that these protests performed the trauma and memory of the disappeared children through embodiment and materiality. That is, the material evidence performed in and of itself. The "bioperformativity," of the DNA, clothes, pictures, and the cells and bacteria embedded in these objects, proves (and performs) the existence of the disappeared children. This evidence fused with the Abuelas and Madres physical presence at the public protests materially entwined the past and the present.

In a similar way, the dancers in *Las Mariposas* performed the story of the Mirabal sisters with the ecological materiality of the past embedded into their bodies, connecting them with the Dominican Republic's geography. Evidence of the violence that Trujillo and his government enacted on the Mirabal sisters (and countless others) endures within the land. While *Las Mariposas* is a performance that takes place on a more traditional stage (based on real people and events), and the political protests of Abuelas and Madres de Plaza de Mayo are events that Taylor analyzes through the framework of performance, they both grapple with the material consequences and "bioperformitivity" of violent Latin American regimes and state terrorism.[7] Discussing ethical land relations in Latin America, feminist playwright and activist Cherríe Moraga states, "humanity's relation with the earth [is] fundamental

A Dirty Pas De Deux 71

to achieving justice," and "a reciprocally respectful relation with land must include regard for land's memory" (cited in Wald et al. 2019, 20). Memories of the disappeared children are housed in the land and in their belongings. Acknowledging the children's existence through these eco-material remains is a critical aspect of the Abuelas and Madres demands for justice. Too, the dirt in *Las Mariposas* materializes the memories and remains contained within the Dominican landscape, as they coalesce with present dancing bodies. The dancers carry remnants of the violent history of the Dominican Republic on their bodies, possibly including microscopic residue of the those killed by Trujillo's government. The physical and emotional discomfort that the Mirabal sisters experienced through their resistance efforts, their time in prison, and ultimately their death is theatrically represented through the dirt's collision with the dancers' bodies, causing them to become sites of distress and pain (Spalink and Whitlock 2012).[8] The material and narrative presence of the Dominican landscape in *Las Mariposas* emphasize Harrison and Hipchen's claim that Alvarez's work insists that we need to "listen to women … listen to the past, to myths and stories of your own geography" (2013, 18). Like the peat in *The Rite of Spring*, the biogeocultography of the dirt in *Las Mariposas* enacted a performative taphonomy, as disinterred ecological matter altered and affected those in the present. Through its "bioperformativity," the dirt charged the performance space with latent memories and environmental histories of the geography of the Dominican Republic. For Taylor, performances concerned with pain and memory demonstrate that "trauma … addresses and affects everyone. We are (all) here" (2003, 189). The (trauma of the) past is also embedded and embodied in the soil. The dancers and dirt in *Las Mariposas*, narratively and materially, perform the traumatic entanglements of humans and more-than-humans (see Figure 3.4).

Toxicity, "Alterlife," and "Staying with the Trouble"

The "bioperformativity" of the dirt often made it challenging for the dancers to partner with it. The ways in which it affected the dancers' bodies and movements testify to the "trans-corporeality" of bodies. But what are the stakes of these relationships? If hundreds, thousands, perhaps millions of organisms are in constant interplay how does that alter an understanding of human bodies and their interactions in performance, and to a greater extent, in the world? In the following sections, I present two examples of the stakes of "trans-corporeality" and consider how they might alter paradigms of performance.

"Trans-corporeality" is potentially perilous, as demonstrated by Polyvinyl chloride (PVC), a ubiquitous material found in many plastics – bottles, toys, pipes, credit cards, medical equipment, food wrap, etc. Feminist philosopher, Nancy Tuana, discusses the disquieting evidence that exhibits higher cancer

72 *A Dirty* Pas De Deux

Figure 3.4 In "The Cemetery is Beginning to Flower," the ensemble members partner with the dirt and the young sisters perform a dance with the clothing of their older counterparts now buried in the bins. Centro Cultural Mauricio Baez in Santo Domingo, Dominican Republic, Thursday December 1, 2011. Photo by Tim Botsko.

rates in PVC production workers. Studies have shown that those working in PVC production have displayed "significantly increased mortality from cancer deaths, including lung cancer, angiosarcoma (liver cancer), and leukemia" (Tuana 2008, 200). The plastics industry maintains, however, that humans exposed to small amounts of phthalates are not at significant risk for cancer. As Tuana explains, though, at a molecular level, phthalates and vinyl chloride interact with human bodies in complex ways that can result in cancer:

> When such a molecule hits such an organ, [like a lung or liver] it interacts with a receptor, which "recognizes" the molecule as a hormonal component. It then either passes through the membrane into the cell to interact with the DNA or RNA of the cell to either turn on or turn off a genetic process, or it releases a molecule that is part of the receptor that does the same thing. That interaction can lead to cancer.
>
> (Tuana 2008, 201)

PVC molecules move through bodies, carrying the potential to reterritorialize them into toxic bodies. Compounds and chemicals harnessed for production under extractive capitalistic systems assert their vitality in seemingly invisible, but often destructive ways.

A Dirty Pas De Deux 73

Similarly, immunologist Gerald Callahan discusses another organism that has transformed human and other species lives alike: bacteria. Bacteria are everywhere: in dirt and food, on animals, doorknobs. Humans, and more-than-humans, share their entire lives with bacteria. "Bacteria ... account for well over 99 percent of all organisms," maintains Callahan. "Even within the space we call us, bacteria outnumber our cells by a factor of 10. Each of us, by cell number, is roughly 90 percent bacteria" (Callahan 2013, 49). And yet, all it takes is one microscopic organism to radically transform your body. Humans typically only take notice of bacteria in the contexts of illness or death, but everyday humans exchange and acquire thousands of bacteria. As the Covid-19 pandemic has drastically demonstrated, we are all together, humans, more-than-humans, and microscopic organisms. Just as humans absorb PVC chemicals which can create toxicity, the porosity among bodies and bacteria also creates trans-corporeal sites with dangerous potential.

Countless bacteria, microbes, and other invisible ecological matter are present in *Las Mariposas,* affecting and altering bodies. The partnering among dancers and dirt enacts an affective, trans-corporeal biogeocultography. Analyzing these interactions through the theories of Alaimo, Braidotti, and Woynarksi shatters the anthropocentric assumption that only humans perform and affirms posthuman theorist Cary Wolfe's claim that the subject is not always human (2003, 1). While these high-stakes interactions occur on stage during *Las Mariposas*, they are also present in the performance venue. In fact, these trans-corporeal exchanges were of great concern to Andy Lowe, the Theatre-in-Residence Program Director, who oversaw the production of *Las Mariposas* at the La Jolla Playhouse. Regarding the production's use of dirt, he stated,

> When you're in the theatre, [the dirt] goes up, and then it stays there, and it eventually falls down onto other things. And when you have a lot of sensitive equipment, lighting, sound, and so forth, when you have people who are trapped in there with those particulates, that gets very toxic. In a situation with dirt, where you have microbes, critters, spores, fungus, mold, that live in the dirt, and that's just the reality of dirt, you are now inhaling all of that.
>
> (Lowe 2012)

The "trans-corporeality" among dirt and humans contained toxic potential. The biogeocultography of the dirt transforms it into an abject object. Comprised of bacteria, microbes, and spores, the dirt can affect the audience members as well as the dancers. The stakes of bringing dirt into the theatre evoke questions regarding the potential trans-corporeal danger of performance. If dirt, chemicals, and bacteria have the capacity to alter bodies, how does that change our understanding of (the stakes of) performance? How can practitioners and scholars acknowledge and engage the more-than-human in performance with care and conscience, in a manner that also acknowledges difference? The toxic realities created through trans-corporeal relations are what technoscience studies scholar, Michelle Murphy (Métis), designates as "alterlife," which is

> the condition of being already co-constituted by material entanglements with water, chemicals, soil, atmospheres, microbes, and built environments, and also the condition of being open to ongoing becoming. Hence, alterlife is already recomposed, pained, and damaged, but has potentiality nonetheless. If life holds together tensions between violence and possibility, braiding the organic and inorganic, body and land, and resides in the indistinctions between infrastructures and ecologies, recognizing alterlife attends also to openness, to a potential for recomposition that exceeds the ongoing aftermaths.
>
> (2018, 118)

"Alterlife" is the entanglement of bodies (human and more-than-human), matter, and systems that are continually composing and re-composing one another. For Murphy, it is not productive to think of these elements as discrete units (e.g., chemicals, pollutants, and microbes), because it is impossible to extricate them from the systems in which they operate and the ways in which they move and reconstitute. Part of Murphy's scholarship is creating "words, protocols, and methods" that burst "open categories of organism, individual, and body to acknowledge a shared, entangling, and extensive condition of being with capitalism and its racist colonial manifestations," to acknowledge "alterlife" (2017, 497, 498).

As the "trans-corporeality" (and potential toxicity) of the dirt in *Las Mariposas* demonstrates, human and more-than-human beings in performance are not discrete actors, but part of "alterlife." A close reading of *Las Mariposas*, through ecocritical and performance theories, disrupts anthropocentric constructs, exhibits the "bioperformativity" of dirt, and demonstrates that the performer is not always human. If performance and performance practices cannot be disentangled from the systems, infrastructures, and toxic potentials of "alterlife," how might this enmeshment be taken seriously? What "words, protocols, or methods" (Murphy 2017, 497), might performance use to contend with "alterlife?" These are complex and unwieldy questions, the answers to which, as Bellacasa elegantly puts it, "cannot be imagined once [and] for all" (2017, 24). However, it is my hope that this chapter's content and questions urge performance practitioners and scholars to consider the trans-corporeal realities of "alterlife" and create methods and techniques that "stay with the trouble," which requires "learning how to be truly present ... as mortal critters entwined in myriad unfinished configurations of places, times, matters, and meanings" (Haraway 2016, 1).

A Dirty Pas De Deux 75

In the next chapter, I continue exploring the questions posed here, by analyzing the performance practices and choreographic techniques used by Iván-Daniel Espinosa to create the durational Butoh performance *Messengers Divinos: A Meditation on Time, Space, Corporeality, & Consciousness* (2018). I argue that Espinosa implements devising techniques that acknowledge the complex lifecycles of fungi and grapple with an ecological ethics of care.

Notes

1 The descriptions in this chapter are based on a 2011 DVD recording of *Las Mariposas* that I received from Eveoke Dance Theatre.
2 Eveoke Dance Theatre has been on hiatus since 2013, when Artistic Director, Ericka Aisha Moore, announced that the organization needed "time for rest and restructure" (Wood 2013). Eveoke was committed to social justice and providing a space where San Diego residents could access performance and dance classes. Their mission statement confirms, "Eveoke Dance Theatre … cultivates compassionate social action through evocative performance, arts education and community building. To that end, [Eveoke produces] an annual season of original dance theatre works, operate an extensive arts education program aimed at long-term, quality interactions between students and teachers, and provide unique experiences that increase visibility for dance and benefit the diverse San Diego community. With core values of access, intention, and collaboration, Eveoke has produced more than 30 original, socially conscious works throughout San Diego since it was founded in 1994" (Sierra 2011).
3 In honor of the Mirabal sisters, November 25 is observed as a day against gender-based violence. In 2000, the General Assembly of the United Nations officially designated this day as the "International day for the Elimination of Violence Against Women" (United Nations n.d.).
4 The cast of *Las Mariposas* were as follows, Charlene Penner as Butterfly, Nikki Dunnan as Dedé, Adult (in Blue), Anabel Roca as Dedé, Youth (in Blue), Araceli Carrera as Patria, Adult (in Yellow), Diondra Eubanks as Patria, Youth (in Yellow), Jessica Rabanzo-Flores as Minerva, Adult (in Red), Pascalle Rodriguez as Minerva, Youth (in Red), Erika Malone as María Teresa, Adult (in Purple), Piper Dye as María Teresa, Youth (in Purple), and ensemble members Becky Hurt, Shayna Cribbs, Molly Terbovich-Ridenhour, and Bruce Walker.
5 The staff, designers, and crew, for *Las Mariposas*, were as follows: Choreography Ericka Aisha Moore, Dramaturg Catherine Kineavy, Sound Design Ericka Aisha Moore, Scenic Design & Construction Jack Lampl, Touring Stage Manager Evangeline Rose Whitlock, Technical Director/ Lighting Designer David Atchison, Costume Design & Construction Araceli Carrera, Costume Construction Sue Dye, Butterfly & Set Silk Painter Suz Knight, Doll Design & Construction Sarah Karpicus, adapted from the novel and co-created by Erika Malone and Ericka Aisha Moore.
6 For the San Diego productions, the dirt was sourced from San Diego. For the Dominican Republic tour, the dirt was sourced from Santiago, Santo Domingo, and Villa Tapia.
7 I am not trying to collapse the differences between Argentina's Dirty War and Trujillo's regime in the Dominican Republic. Rather, I strive to demonstrate the ways in which Diana Taylor's analysis of the protests of Abuelas and Madres de Plaza de Mayo and my analysis of *Las Mariposas* both grapple with the material consequences and "bioperformitivity," of violent Latin American regimes.
8 I am not saying that the pain experienced by the Mirabal sisters is the same as that experienced by the dancers, clearly it is not. Rather, that the dancer's discomfort dancing with the dirt creates a theatrical representation of the sisters' experiences.

References

Alaimo, Stacy. 1998. "Skin Dreaming: The Bodily Transgressions of Fielding Burke, Octavia Butler, and Linda Hogan" In *Ecofeminist Literary Criticism: Theory, Interpretation, Pedagogy*, edited by Greta Gaard and Patrick D. Murphy, 123–138. Illinois: University of Illinois.

Alaimo, Stacy. 2008. "Trans-corporeal Feminisms and the Ethical Space of Nature." In *Material Feminisms*, edited by Stacy Alaimo and Susan Hekman, 237–264. Bloomington: Indiana University Press.

Alvarez, Julia. 1994. *In the Time of the Butterflies*. Chapel Hill: Algonquin Books of Chapel Hill.

Barbas-Rhoden, Laura. 2019."Gendering EcoHispanisms: Knowledge, Gender, and Place in a Pluricultural Latin America." In *Hispanic Ecocriticism*, edited by José Manuel Marrero Henríquez, 69–93. Berlin: Peter Lang Publishing.

Bellacasa, María Puig de la. 2017. *Matters of Care*. Minneapolis: University of Minneapolis Press.

Braidotti, Rosi. 2006. *Transpositions: On Nomadic Ethics*. Cambridge: Polity Press.

Callahan, Gerald N. 2013. *Lousy Sex: Creating Self in an Infectious World*. Boulder: University Press of Colorado.

Croce, Arelene. 1984. "Bausch's Theatre of Dejection." In *The Pina Bausch Sourcebook: The Making of Tanztheater*, edited by Royd Climenhaga, 192–195. New York: Routledge.

Deleuze, Gilles. 1993. "Rhizome Versus Trees." In *The Deleuze Reader*, edited by Constantin V. Boundas. New York: Columbia University Press.

Deleuze, Gilles and Felix Guattari. 1987. *A Thousand Plateaus: Capitalism and Schizophrenia*. Minneapolis: University of Minnesota Press.

Douglas, Mary. 1966. *Purity and Danger: An Analysis of the Concepts of Pollution and Taboo*. London: Ark Paperbacks.

Eveoke Dance Theatre. 2011. *Las Mariposas*. DVD.

Gómez-Barris, Macarena. 2017. *The Extractive Zone: Social Ecologies and Decolonial Perspectives*. Durham: Duke University Press.

Grice, Elizabeth A., Heidi H. Kong, Sean Conlan, Clayton B. Deming, Joie Davis, Alice C. Young, Gerard G. Bouffard, Robert W. Blakesley, Patrick R. Murray, Eric D. Green, Maria L. Turner, and Julia A. Segre. 2009. "Topographical and Temporal Diversity of the Human Skin Microbiome." *Science* 324: 1190–1192.

Harrison, Rebecca L., and Emily Hipchen. 2013. "Introduction." In *Inhabiting La Patria: Identity, Agency, and Antojo in the Work of Julia Alvarez*, edited by Rebecca L. Harrison and Emily Hipchen, 1–20. Albany: SUNY Press.

Henríquez, José Manuel Marrero. 2019. *Hispanic Ecocriticism*. Edited by José Manuel Marrero Henríquez., Berlin: Peter Lang Publishing.

Haraway, Donna J. 2016. *Staying with the Trouble*. Durham: Duke University Press.

"International Day for the Elimination of Violence against Women 25 November." *United Nations*, n.d. United Nations. Accessed July 27, 2022. https://www.un.org/en/observances/ending-violence-against-women-day/background#:~:text=Women's%20rights%20activists%20have%20observed,Trujillo%20(1930%2D1961).

Johnson, Kelli Lyon. 2005. *Julia Alvarez: Writing a New Place on the Map*. Albuquerque: University of New Mexico Press.

Kane, Adrian Taylor. 2014. "Preface." In *The Natural World in Latin American Literatures: Ecocritical Essays on Twentieth Century Writings*, edited by Adrian Taylor Kane, 1–8. Jefferson: McFarland.

Kristeva, Julia. 1982. *Powers of Horror*. Translated by Louis-Ferdinand Celine. New York: Columbia University Press.
Lowe, Andy. 2012. Interview by Evangeline Rose Whitlock. MP3 recording. San Diego, California. March. 22, 2012.
Moore, Ericka Aisha. 2012. Interview by Evangeline Rose Whitlock. MP3 recording. San Diego, California. January 17, 2012.
Murphy, Michelle. 2017. "Alterlife and Decolonial Chemical Relations." *Cultural Anthropology* 32, no. 4: 494–503.
Murphy, Michelle. 2018. "Against Population, Towards Alterlife." In *Making Kin Not Population*, edited by Adele E. Clarke and Donna Haraway, 101–124. Cambridge: Prickly Paradigm Press.
Nardi, James B. 2007. *Life in the Soil: A Guide for Naturalists and Gardeners*. Chicago: The University of Chicago Press.
Noske, Barbara. 1989. *Humans and Other Animals: Beyond the Boundaries of Anthropology*. London: Pluto Press.
Ress, Mary Judith. 2006. *Ecofeminism in Latin America*. Maryknoll: Orbis Books.
Sierra, Gabrielle. 2011. "La Jolla Playhouse Announces 2011/12 Resident Theatre Company." *Broadway World San Diego*. March 28, 2011.
Spalink, Angenette and Evangeline Rose Whitlock. 2012. "'And so I offered them our Land': The Land/Body Intersection in Eveoke Dance Theatre's *Las Mariposas*," Presentation at the Earth Matters on Stage conference. Pittsburgh, Pennsylvania.
Taylor, Diana. 2003. *The Archive and the Repertoire*. Durham: Duke University Press.
Tuana, Nancy. 2008. "Viscous Porosity: Witnessing Katrina." In *Material Feminisms*, edited Stacy Alaimo and Susan Hekman, 188–213. Bloomington: Indiana University Press.
Walker, Bruce, Becky Hurt, Molly Terbovich-Ridenhour, and Shayna Cribbs. 2012. Interview by Evangeline Rose Whitlock. MP3 recording. San Diego, California. January 31, 2012.
Wald, Sarah D., David J. Vazquez, Priscilla Solis Ybarra, and Sarah Jaquette Ray. 2019. "Introduction: Why Latinx Environmentalisms?" In *Latinx Environmentalisms: Place, Justice, and the Decolonial*, edited by Sarah D. Wald, David J. Vazquez, Priscilla Solis Ybarra, and Sarah Jaquette Ray, 1–34. Philadelphia: Temple University Press.
Wolfe, Cary. 2003. *Animal Rites: American Culture, the Discourse of Species, and Posthumanist Theory*. Chicago: The University of Chicago Press.
Wood, Beth. 2013. "Eveoke Dance Theatre to Close." *The San Diego Union Tribune*. August 11, 2013.
Woynarski, Lisa. 2020. *Ecodramaturgies: Theatre, Performance and Climate Change*. Switzerland: Palgrave Macmillan.

4 Mycelium in Motion
Choreographing Care in Iván-Daniel Espinosa's *Messengers Divinos*

I walk into a small, dark theatre in the Midtown Arts & Theatre Center in Houston, Texas and the first thing I notice is the odor. The theatre smells like manure. I maneuver to my seat and identify from where the smell is emanating – a substantial heap of dirt and fungi located downstage center. The dirt is in clumps and different fungi are emerging from it. Some look like classical mushrooms with brown caps and stems, others resemble corals, white frills of lace, or fibrous filaments. While the vegetal performance of the fungi is ongoing, the human performance begins. Two dancers, coated in a chalky, dirt-like substance, appear upstage right and left. Their movement is unhurried, intricate, and precise. They slowly travel downstage toward the dirt and fungi. When they arrive, they touch the fungi (and by extension the dirt), caress it, hold it, move with it, and place it on their bodies. The humans appear to exercise care and attentiveness as they dance with the fungi, regarding it with the same gravity as another human performer (see Figure 4.1). As the performance continues, the fungi and dirt are no longer concentrated to a pile downstage. They move throughout the entire stage area as they perform with the human dancers. *Messengers Divinos: A Meditation on Time, Space, Corporeality, & Consciousness* (2018) was choreographed and directed by Iván-Daniel Espinosa.[1] This durational Butoh performance incorporated mycological research into the choreography to create movement that partnered humans and mycelium – networks of fungi – by situating them "skin to skin, pore to pore" (Program 2018).

Up to this point, *Choreographing Dirt* has focused on the biogeocultography of ecological matter, how it alters other bodies, as well as its vitality and "bioperformativity" (Woynarski 2020). *The Rite of Spring* and *Las Mariposas* each employed varying degrees of ecological awareness in their incorporation of dirt and peat. Ecocritical analyses of these performances exhibit the extractive logics of capitalism which create toxic potentials for trans-corporeal beings. This chapter, however, takes a slight veer to consider how performance practices might incorporate (speculative) ecological ethics. Incorporating some of the questions that emerged from previous

DOI: 10.4324/9781003164234-5

Figure 4.1 Dancers and fungi performing in *Messengers Divinos* (2018) at the Seattle International Butoh Festival. Photo by Jim Lee Carey.

chapters, this chapter queries: How can practitioners and scholars engage with more-than-human beings in performance, with care and conscience, in a manner that also acknowledges difference? What "methods" might performance use to contend with "alterlife?" (Murphy 2017, 497). To consider these questions, I execute a close reading of *Messengers Divinos*' devising methods, sound design, and performances. Analyzing *Messengers Divinos* through the theories of María Puig de la Bellacasa and Dwayne Trevor Donald, I contend that *Messengers Divinos* engages the heterogeneous temporalties of fungi and utilizes techniques that focus on relationality. I also utilize Bellacasa's concepts of haptic encounters and mundane actions to argue that *Messengers Divinos* grapples with an ecological ethics of care. This type of care is not fully realized in many performance practices. *Messengers Divinos* operates as praxis for creating performance and dance in ethical and relational ways that are more attuned to the diverse array of more-than-human performers.

Animals, Plants, and Fungi – Oh My!

Conventional performance in the west often relegates the more-than-human to the margins of the stage, so to speak. Animals, plants, fungi, and other ecological matter tend to be considered inferior to humans, despite scientific research demonstrating their intelligence (Gagliano et al. 2020; Stamets 2005).

While eco-performance has made strides to de-center the human, establishing interspecies theories and practices, this scholarship often focuses on animals, particularly charismatic megafauna. As environmental humanities scholar Courtney Ryan points out,

> While animal studies continues to consider what these new [performance] practices might be, theatre scholarship on human engagement with flora remains underexplored. Plants, in particular, have received far less attention from the humanities, even though humans are arguably more dependent on plants than they are on animals.
>
> (2013, 337)

Ryan identifies that while scholarship on animal performance burgeons, plant performance is underdeveloped even though plants perform in manifold ways. Environmental humanities scholars, Prudence Gibson and Catriona Sandilands, explain that plants perform "in their own interests [and] as part of a multispecies network of performativity in which ... showiness, smelliness, and eventfulness combine in specific ways to bring about desired ends such as pollination" (2021, 2). Humans can perceive plant performance through aesthetics, sensorial perceptions, and spatiality (plant growth). However, it is difficult for humans to perceive how dirt and fungi perform, as these performances are often microscopic and occur in heterogeneous temporalities. If plant performance is overlooked, then fungi, dirt, and other ecological matter are perhaps even more disregarded. My intent here is not to minimize the importance of animal studies or the developing field of critical plant studies; but rather to expand performance scholarship and practices to consider how dirt, peat, fungi, bacteria, protozoa, etc. can be understood through a performance framework. These more-than-human beings indeed perform in their own interests and sometimes also perform in ways that humans can perceive.

In many ways *Messengers Divinos* animates anthropologist Anna Lowenhaupt Tsing's claim that places of decomposition generate multispecies life and offer ways to reconsider relationships among humans and more-than-humans (2015, 6). Many fungi are saprophytic, meaning they can decompose organic matter. Decomposition plays a significant role in many ecosystems. As mycologist Paul Stamets confirms, fungi "recycle carbon, hydrogen, nitrogen... and other minerals into nutrients for living plants insects, and other organisms sharing that habitat" (2005, 19). Fungi's ability to decompose, recycle, and reassemble organic matter is critical to the subsistence of certain environments. Through death and decomposition, fungi sustain a myriad of multispecies life. Therefore, mycelial ecosystems are great places to rethink multispecies relationships within the context of performance. *Messengers Divinos*, then, is a fecund site to consider the performance of fungi and an ecological ethics of performance.

Messengers Divinos

A small cluster of dancers lay on their backs with their legs extended toward the ceiling, feet flat, toes flexed. They are wearing gossamer slips or dance belts and are covered in what appears to be dried mud. Their legs bend as they begin to slowly bring their feet down to the ground. The movement is not fluid, but extremely slow, occurring in fits and starts. The bodies are never still, as they constantly execute micro-movements and adjustments. With their backs on the ground, the dancers begin to tilt their heads back, using them to push against the floor. This force pushes their pelvises toward the ceiling and transitions their bodies into bridge pose. Slowly they move into sitting positions and form a circle around the dirt and fungi that also occupy the space. The dancers extend their arms out to the fungi and touch it. Eventually, they begin moving with the fungi, partnering with it in various ways (see Figure 4.2). Three dancers stand up. One dancer remains on the floor in child's pose with their arms horizontally extended. The three standing dancers hold the fungi and gently sprinkle it onto the back of the dancer in child's pose. The fungi slowly accumulate on the dancer's back.

Latino choreographer and experimental dance artist, Iván-Daniel Espinosa, integrates environmental philosophy with sound studies and dance to create interdisciplinary work that explores connections among humans and earthy landscapes. In *Messengers Divinos,* performed at the Houston Fringe Festival (2018), Seattle Butoh Festival (2018), and New York City's La

Figure 4.2 Fungi, dirt, and dancers in *Messengers Divinos* (2018) at the Seattle International Butoh Festival. Photo by Jim Lee Carey.

MaMa Experimental Theatre Club (2018), Espinosa uses choreography and bio-sonification to explore the somatic and sonic relations among fungi and humans.[2] *Messengers Divinos* is a multisensory experience. The performers and audience can see, hear, and smell the fungi (and dirt). Mycological research demonstrates that mycelia are sentient; they can sense, hear, and feel other forms of life, including humans (Olsson and Hansson 1995, Stamets 2005). Centering mycelia's sentience was a critical aspect of Espinosa's choreographic investigations. His devising process queried, "what [does] it take to slow down and notice the vibrant matter that lies so close at hand?" (Fringe Festival 2018). To explore this question, he implemented Butoh exercises that empowered the dancers to open themselves to sensing mycelium. The intersections of mycology, Butoh, and durational performance created a spatiotemporality where the dancers could attune to the sentience and lifecycles of mycelium. The next section focuses on Dwayne Trevor Donald's "Indigenous Métissage" (2009) and María Puig de la Bellacasa's speculative ethics of care (2017), discussing how each offers an approach to ecological relationality and ethics. In the section that follows, I apply these theories to Espinosa's Butoh practice to demonstrate how the devising process and performance of *Messengers Divinos* activates an eco-relationality.

Ecological Relationality and "Temporalities of Care"

Elucidating how colonization violently severs people from place in the context of "Aboriginal-Canadian relations," education scholar, Dwayne Trevor Donald (Papaschase Cree), presents the story of a particular rock known to the Cree as *papamihaw asiniy* or *flying rock* (2009, 1). He first explains that for the Plains Cree, rocks are,

> animate entities, [they] have an energy to them that is forever in flux – constantly changing, transforming, combining and recombining. This cyclic energy is what gives the rock its spiritual quality. When one sees the world in this way there are two general premises that result. One is that the constant flux process of energy means that everything is related through the cyclic nature of energy flows. The second is that we must look at the world holistically and search for regular observable patterns in nature as a way to make sense of the world and our place in it.
>
> (Donald 2009, 14)

Rocks are vital, spiritual entities that have deep connections with people and place. Regarding the *papamihaw asiniy*, it was designated as such because it fell/flew from the sky to earth, and its location became a scared site of pilgrimage for both the Cree and Blackfoot (Donald 2009, 1). The *papamihaw asiniy* was stolen by John McDougall, a Methodist missionary, sometime in the 1800s. After its initial removal, it was housed in Royal Museum of Ontario and then eventually moved to the Royal Alberta Museum, where it still resides. Its initial theft by McDougall and current residence at the Royal Alberta Museum enact colonial ecological violence as the rock's displacement separates it from its sacred geography and reduces it to an object devoid of vitality and spirituality.

The story of the *papamihaw asiniy* exhibits how colonial practices continue to "enforce epistemological and social conformity to Eurowestern standards," where matter is reduced to a resource (Donald 2009, 2–4). To counter this colonial, social, and ecological violence, Donald presents "Indigenous Métissage," "an ecological understanding of... relationality that does not deny difference, but rather seeks to more deeply understand how our different histories and experiences position us in relation to each other" (2009, 6). "Indigenous Métissage" is grounded in an ethical reorganization of relations among place, people, matter, and objects that recognizes their intricate enmeshment – which includes dimensions of spirituality and animacy – and does not deny difference. This practice requires that "we... pay closer attention to interactions which always are imbued with a living principle of reciprocity, and hence moral responsibility for a shared future" (Donald 2009, 8–9). Because we exist in a relational web, the prosaic interactions among humans, rocks, rivers, plants, and fungi matter, and require careful attunement.

Feminist philosopher, María Puig de la Bellacasa, also contends that our current epoch requires "an ethical reorganization of human-nonhuman relations," as many exploitative and violent ecological practices are the result of settler colonialism and colonialism (2017, 24). Donald's practice of "Indigenous Métissage" is situated within Cree cosmology and Bellacasa's within a western worldview. While theorized within different ontologies and not identical, both of their concepts focus on relationality and acknowledgment of difference. Bellacasa formulates a speculative ethics of care as something that circulates in both human and more-than-human realms and "[enacts] nonexploitative forms of togetherness" (2017, 24). Using human-soil relations as a case study for a "temporalities of care" that disrupts anthropocentrism, she examines how "alternative practical, ethical, and affective ecologies of care are emerging that trouble the traditional direction of progress and the speed of technoscientific, productionist, future-driven interventions" (2017, 23).

Bellacasa anchors her conception of care in human-soil relations because soil has garnered attention as a resource exhausted by technoscience that is "in need of urgent care" (2017, 13). Delving into the history of soil science, she examines historically situated conceptions of soil, noting that "it is only since the mid-nineteenth century that scientific developments in chemistry physics, and biology, coalesce into the interdisciplinary field of soil sciences" (2017, 172). While acknowledging diverse approaches to soil science, Bellacasa argues that many soil science methods, particularly in the global north, align soil fertility with production demand. This productionist logic converges soil science and economics to emphasize yield. Concerned with efficiency and production, this logic treats soil as a mechanism to grow crops. Thus, many soil science methods reduce both soil and crops to economic resources. Bellacasa argues that this productionist logic "is a form of exploitative and instrumentally regimented care, orientated by a one-way anthropocentric temporality" (2017, 186). She presents, "temporalities of care," "the pace required by ecological relations with soil," to counter to the linear temporality of production (Bellacasa 2017, 23). "Temporalities of care" are embodied through the foodweb model, where soil is understood as a living relational community.

In the 1990s, foodweb models of soil relations became prominent as some scientists believed that they better captured the "complex interactions between species that allow the circulation of nutrients and energy" (Bellacasa 2017, 191). Foodwebs are comprised of a diverse array of species, including algae, mycelium, bacteria, earthworms, plants, animals, and humans. They each perform various tasks such as nutrient exchange and decomposition. Mycelia are significant components of soils, and the composition of entire ecosystems can depend on their resident fungi. In fact, one cubic inch of topsoil can contain enough fungal cells to extend about 8 miles (Stamets 2005, 10). Scientists in microbial ecology are just beginning to understand the profound impacts of these symbiotic relationships among fungi, plants, and the soil. Stamets attests that "fungi are keystone species that create ever-thickening layers of soil, which allow future plant and animal generations to flourish. Without fungi, all ecosystems would fail" (2005, 1).

The foodweb model situates humans as members of an enmeshed community of soil, fungi, mycelium, and many other species. Bellacasa explains that this model unsettles anthropocentrism by disrupting "the unidirectionality of care conceived within the linear timescapes of productionist time traditionally centered in human-crop relations" (2017, 191). The relationality of species centered in the foodweb enacts "temporalities of care" because ecological relations require heterogeneous temporalities, as decomposition, nutrient cycling, growth and decay of flora and fauna, and the movement of water and gasses through the soil, all occur on different timescales. In this model, soil is not a resource for humans, but rather, a vital member of a multispecies web, with which humans are in-relation. In the next section, I examine how Butoh enabled Espinosa to explore relationality and "temporalities of care" among humans and mycelium.

Butoh and Mycelium

Espinosa used Butoh techniques to choreograph *Messengers Divinos* because the intentionality and experimental nature of Butoh provided generative methods to explore the spatiotemporal relations among humans and mycelium. Butoh materialized in 1960s Japan through the dance experiments of

Hijikata Tatsumi and Ohno Kazuo. Influenced by German modern dance, "Japanese and European surrealism… [and] modernist and avant-garde literature and painting," Butoh is considered "a major innovation in 20th century dance and performance" (Baird and Candelario 2019, 1). It was through Butoh that Espinosa first encountered mycelium. He vividly recounts the experience,

> I danced in the forest and… I tripped over a log… And I noticed that there were these giant yellow mushrooms growing… off of the log… and then I… noticed that there was this… white spider web-like material deep inside of the log. I was… close with these mushroom bodies [because] Butoh encourages the dancer to use their body in unconventional ways, in non-normative ways. So up is down and down is up and you're … upside down and you're rolling on the ground and you're crawling like a spider. Those are very common approaches in a lot of Butoh exercises. So, I was crawling all over this log and, and just looking deep inside of it. And that's when I noticed the spider web material. I realized, Oh my goodness, this … is the mycelium that I had read about… but I had never seen it. I didn't know what it looked like; I didn't know what it felt like. I never confronted it so magically.
>
> (Espinosa 2020)

The non-normative movement of Butoh enabled Espinosa to encounter the mycelium. This experience piqued a curiosity in fungi attunement that he developed in *Messengers Divinos*. For Espinosa, the ontology of Butoh was well aligned with an ecological relationality. As he explains, Butoh exhibits "an ontology of the body that is inherently connected to and entangled with all of the dynamic ecosystems that we move and walk through, from the tiniest mushroom to the tallest tree" (2018). Butoh techniques create space for transcorporeal explorations in performance.

In rehearsals, Espinosa used the Butoh concept of the "sponge body," to encourage the dancers to conceive of their bodies as porous and enmeshed with the environment. As he explicates,

> the idea is that you imagine your entire body from head to toe as a giant sponge. And every time that you inhale and take a deep breath in, you are absorbing the environment through the pores in your skin. You … absorb the environment and you absorb the non-human world, and it enters your, your body, it enters your being and it mixes with… everything that's going on in there, and it becomes a part of you.
>
> (Espinosa 2020)

As discussed in previous chapters, the human body is not discrete, but rather a porous assemblage that constantly shifts and changes as it encounters other beings and environments. The "sponge body" allowed the dancers to shift their perception of their bodies from discrete to permeable. Espinosa expounds,

> The body does not exist as mass that moves in the already existing space. Rather, the space is defined as my body [plus] the environment, where the self is a kind of transient membrane, and the space is perceived by passing through the human body. The 'body itself' becomes more-than and other-than 'itself' with infinite potential for all kinds of transformations, recompositions and reconfigurations.
>
> (2018)

Implementing this embodied knowledge into the choreography was a critical step for the dancers that allowed them to expand their sensations. The "sponge body" unsettles the human from an anthropocentric hierarchy, as human performers understand their corporeal forms as enmeshed with the mycelium. Much like the foodweb, the "sponge body," expanded the performers awareness to be in-relation to the mycelium. The mycelium was not a resource or prop, but a vital performer in the dance. The dancers attuned themselves to the movements, sounds, and affects of the mycelium, just as they would another human. This physical and cognitive reorganization of human and mycelial interactions exhibited a sensibility of ethical relationality. Unlike the dancers in *Las Mariposas*, the dancers in *Messengers Divinos* never articulated a struggle working with the fungi or getting "dirty." This could be due, in part, to a difference in trainings. The dancers in *Las Mariposas* were predominantly trained in traditional western concert dance traditions. The dancers in *Messengers Divinos* were trained in Butoh and perhaps more accustomed to working in site-specific spaces with more-than-human partners.

While the "sponge body" counters anthropocentrism through eco-relationality, the durational nature of the performance and extremely slow movements of the choreography enact "temporalties of care" that counter capitalist productionist time. By unfolding over an extended period – performances have lasted up to five hours – *Messengers Divinos* allowed the dancers to practice intentional interactions with the fungi. Although slowness is not inherent to all Butoh practices, it was crucial to Espinosa's choreography as this tempo allowed the dancers to explore a temporality grounded in relationality. Espinosa specified that the slowness allowed the dancers to "sustain [an] ... energetic focus and intensity," in their bodies that enabled them to move "in ways that diverge from the human norm," and "[engage] with time and space differently" (2020). He observed that the duration and tempo effected the dancers "physical spatiotemporal dynamic" (Espinosa 2020). After performing for several hours, the dancers told him, "wow, we're really relating to the mycelia, we're seeing things we didn't see before" (Espinosa 2020). Through duration and intentional slowness, the dancers countered capitalist productionist time through "temporalties of care" that enabled them to relationally attune to the mycelium.

Haptic Encounters

For humans to conceive of an ethics of care within the foodweb (and by extension the more-than-human world), Bellacasa contends that they must understand these interactions as both reciprocal and nonreciprocal. She explains,

> Reciprocity of care is asymmetric and multilateral, collectively shared. A caring conception of soil emphasizes this embeddedness in relations of interdependence. Caring for soil communities involves making a speculative effort toward the acknowledgement that the human carer also depends on soil's capacity to 'take care' of a number of processes that are vital to more than her existence.

(2017, 192)

Humans must acknowledge their imbrication in systems where they are cared for by other beings and species. Donald also emphasizes the imperative of humans recognizing their embeddedness in the more-than-human world (2009, 7). "[Human and more-than-human] histories and experiences are layered and position us in relation to each other"; therefore, our futures will always be entangled, contends Donald (2009, 7). For those situated in western ontologies, a speculative leap to recognize care as present in the more-than-human world requires an ontological shift. Soil, mycelium, bacteria, flora, fauna, and humans all care for one another, in irregular and manifold ways. For Bellacasa, haptic engagements – seeing, touching, hearing, being-with, and learning about ecological matter – empower humans to make this speculative leap. These encounters are not hinged on identification. Humans do not need to recognize human characteristics or traits in more-than-humans to care. Rather, haptic experiences "[engage] curiosity toward a web of doings, obligations, and asymmetrical reciprocities that [people] can easily conceive: the soil you depend on depends on those who depend on you" (Bellacasa 2017, 199). While not identical to Donald's understanding of ethical relationality, which does not deny difference "but rather seeks to more deeply understand how our different histories and experiences position us in relation to each other" (2009, 6), both theorizations recognize the significance of relationality and care. These practices enable humans to reconsider their place within the material and ontological web of existence. The following sections examine haptic encounters of sight, sound, and touch/eating in *Messengers Divinos*, contending that they exhibit a speculative ethics of care in the performance.

Sight

The darkness slowly fades, and a large cluster of glistening white and brown mushrooms (the fruiting bodies of fungi) appear on the back wall of the theatre. The mushrooms have slender stems and flat segmented caps. They expand quickly. As they grow, the focus sharpens. Suddenly, they disappear, and different mushrooms appear. These ones are matte white, thick, and long, with a bumpy texture. There is a profuse amount of them, growing from a single base. They expand and extend, taking up more and more space. Their convex caps, barely visible at the beginning, widen significantly, becoming concave as they broaden out.

These time-lapse films of various fungi lifecycles were projected onto the back wall during *Messengers Divinos*, enabling audiences to view fungi developing, growing, and decaying – processes that occur over multiple temporalties. Exhibiting these perpetual processes in time-lapse was important to Espinosa because he wanted to "[show] images of decomposition and … decay because that's very important in the life cycle of fungi and, well, of all of us" (2020). Humans are not typically privy to these processes because they occur in multiple temporalties. Time-lapse, which captures these cycles on film, speeds them up and presents them linearly, which allows humans to visually perceive them. While these heterogeneous fungi temporalities were filtered through a linear human temporality, this can be understood as "ecological anthropomorphism" (Woynarski 2015, 24). An ecologically anthropomorphic reading of the projections foregrounds the temporalties of the fungi, allowing humans to experience aspects of fungi lifecycles that are typically inaccessible.

Espinosa incorporated the projections in case audiences were unable to see the intricacies of the fungi choreography. He stated, "at least if [the audience] can't see the dancers … maybe they can watch the screen … and at least understand, 'oh, right now we are meditating on expansion and growth and blooming and fruiting'" (2020). Sight was a significant aspect of the performance's haptic engagement. Espinosa wanted the audience to see both the partnering among humans and fungi and the fungi processes that occur in heterogeneous temporalities. Seeing both the myopic and hyperopic interactions emphasized the intricate lifecycles of fungi that are often invisible to humans. The projections and the choreography offered a haptic encounter for the performers and audience. It allowed them to see fungi lifecycles in the performance but also in the broader context of the relational web of life. By centering fungi temporalities, *Messengers Divinos* exhibited how decomposition and other fungi cycles are integral to the foodweb.

Sound

A low-pitched pulsating sustained rhythm
Discordant electrical beeping
Wind blowing
Buzzing
Ambient noise
A low drone
High-pitched static sounds

These are some of the discernable sounds – ranging in tone from ambient to dissonant – resounding throughout the space during *Messengers Divinos*. The soundscape, co-created by Espinosa, was a sonic mix of fungi and other sounds.[3] Espinosa remarked that as a choreographer, he is "curious about how soundscapes in live performance can engage, both socially and somatically, with the bodies of 'more-than-human' beings" (2018). In the case of *Messenger Divinos,* he wanted to make the internal responses of the fungi audible to humans, but he was also curious if the fungi would be able sense themselves in the soundscape. To create the soundscape, he connected mushrooms "to motion sensors and electrical connectors that [perceived] the electromagnetic variations from the surface of mushroom caps to the root system of the mycelium and [translated] them to sounds" (Fringe Festival 2018). Mycelia are sentient and able to sense the presence of others in their environment. They can send information about what they sense to other lifeforms in their habitat. Research conducted by ecologists Stefan Olsson and B.S. Hansson establishes that "fungus can use electrical signals to send messages between different mycelial parts, messages conveying information regarding food sources, injury, local conditions... or the presence of other individuals" (1995, 30). Because of their ability to communicate, Stamets refers to mycelium as "biomolecular superhighways," because they are "in constant dialogue with [their] environment" (2005, 7). This communication is predominantly unintelligible to humans. However, a 2022 study conducted by computer scientist Andrew Adamatzky utilized math and linguistic theory to calculate the number of "words" used by four different fungal species. The study found "that size of fungal lexicon can be up to 50 words; however, the core lexicon of most frequently used words does not exceed 15–20 words" (Adamatzky 2022, 13).

Espinosa wanted to center the mycelium's sentience so dancers and spectators could experience the mycelium's vitality and intelligence. For the New York City performance, Espinosa worked with musician Omer Gal to attach bio-sonification devices, which sense bioelectric changes, to fungal colonies. The bio-sonification devices registered a change in bioelectricity when humans touched the mycelium (Espinosa 2020). Discussing this process, Espinosa explained how the fungi responded to human touch with a beeping sound.

> Some of the fungi species respond much more than others, and they all respond in different ways ... like Turkey Tail fungi ... respond like with [a] long drone... but cordyceps mushrooms ... [respond] very quickly. They're like [faster beeping noises] beepbeepbeepbeep. All of the different species respond differently when they're touched by humans. And then when the human stops touching them, their response changes as well.
>
> (2020)

The fungi sensed and responded to changes in their environment and human touch. The bio-sonification devices allowed humans to hear these responses but did not clarify (in a human language) what the responses meant or what the fungi were communicating.

Espinosa used these sounds to create the soundscape for *Messenger Divinos*, which he identified as cyborg because "it's their own [the fungi] sound, but... it's manipulated. It's mediated, it's tampered with, so... it's like a hybrid sound" (2020). He described it as "very arresting and ... very loud... it's not a gentle soundscape" (Espinosa 2020). Because of its intensity, the sound really engulfs the space and creates an immersive experience. Since many fungi processes occur in heterogeneous temporalities and mycelium connects under the soil, fungi are often associated with stillness and quietude as humans cannot sense their movements and lifecycles. As Leila Fadel, host of NPR's "Morning Edition," stated during a segment on fungi, "Mushrooms – they keep to themselves [and] don't move around" (2022). Creating a soundscape that foregrounds fungi's ability to communicate by exhibiting their somatic and sonic capabilities counters the notion of fungi as quiet static objects. For the Houston and New York City performances, the soundscapes were recorded. For the Seattle performance, though, the soundscape was live. Bio-sonification devices were attached to the fungi in this performance. So, the sounds of the fungi responding to the dancer's touch were occurring in real time and amplified for the audience.

The soundscape centered on the sentience, vitality, and temporalties of the fungi. These processes, inaudible to humans, were made audible (to humans) through bio-sonification and used to create the soundscape. Espinosa was also intrigued by the possibility that the mycelium could hear themselves in the soundscape. If they could hear themselves, how would this change their responses in the performance? (Espinosa 2020). While we cannot definitively know if the fungi heard themselves in the soundscape and responded, we can surmise that if they are sentient and sensitive to their surrounding environment, then perhaps they did hear themselves. If so, then the mycelium were somatic and sonic collaborators in the performance.

Mycelium in Motion 91

Touch/Eat

A dancer kneels behind a brown and white fungus. It has cylindric branches with ruffled edges that extend vertically. The dancer stretches their arms toward the fungi, then bows their head and crouches down to the floor. When they raise their head back up, they are holding a large mushroom in their mouth (see Figure 4.3). They close their eyes and crouch down again. They eventually raise their head back up and begin to stand, the mushroom still gently held in their mouth. With their head slightly tilted toward the ceiling and their eyes still closed, they begin chewing. Tilting their head back further, they stretch their arms toward the ceiling and continue to chew. Once the mushroom is completely consumed, the dancer opens their eyes and looks up toward the ceiling. There is a smudge of dirt on their forehead and their face is dotted with sweat. Their arms gradually descend, and they place their hands on their chest in the area where their heart resides.

Ingestion and expulsion are crucial to the reproductive lifecycle of fungi, and therefore, consuming mushrooms was a significant aspect of preparing for *Messengers Divinos*. Mycologist Willie Crosby told Espinosa that mushrooms want to be eaten because that is how they spread their spores.[4] Animals (and humans) eat mushrooms and then expel them into soil as waste. Once in the soil, the spores begin to germinate. Crosby affirmed Espinosa's desire to consume mushrooms in the performance, stating, "trust me, they [mushrooms] want to be eaten because that's how they spread and take over the

Figure 4.3 A dancer consuming fungi in *Messengers Divinos* (2018) at the Seattle International Butoh Festival. Photo by Jim Lee Carey.

forest... and travel to new lands" (cited in Espinosa 2020). Mushrooms are consumed during the performance, as detailed in the opening description of this section, but Espinosa also had performers drink mushroom tea beforehand. Drinking mushroom tea became a pre-show ritual. Espinosa explains that "if we're working with Reishi and Chaga mushrooms, I have them drink Reishi and Chaga tea ... [then] it's in our body. It's swimming in our blood, and now we're dancing with the thing that nourished us" (2020). The mushrooms reside within them as they perform.

The "sponge body" allowed the dancers be in-relation to the fungi physically, while consuming the mushroom tea altered the interiority of their bodies and their gut microbiota. The mushrooms become part of the dancers' bodies. They collaborated with the fungi externally and internally. The mushrooms desire to be eaten (according to Crosby) corresponds with the food-web cycle of consumption, expulsion, decay, and growth. "Participants in the foodweb must... embody the time of the cycle by eating or becoming food for other participants in the death and decay cycle," asserts Bellacasa (2017, 202). "Immersion in a foodweb as life politics creates specific practical eco-ethical obligations, such as the cyclic return of organic waste" (Bellacasa 2017, 202). Through drinking and eating the mushrooms, the dancers become part of the foodweb, participating in processes of death, decay, and life. As performance scholar Clara Margaret Wilch attests, *Messengers Divinos* demonstrates the ways in which "life and death are in coexistence and mutual exchange, where decomposition can be experienced sensorily" (2020, 67). Through the haptic acts of touching and eating, the dancers practice a life politics of "eco-ethical obligations." Fungi care for the dancers through nourishment, while the dancers care for fungi by centering its lifecycles and temporalities.

When the performance was over, the unconsumed fungi were returned. Some fungi were sourced from scientific labs, while others were transferred from a forest. The fungi returned to the forest can reconnect with its original mycelial networks (Espinosa 2020). Microbial ecologist Yu Fukasawa's research on mycelium's ability to reestablish itself in habitats demonstrates that fungi exhibit "decision making" in determining where to send their mycelia when placed in a new environment (Fukasawa et al. 2020). By reestablishing in an environment, fungi can resume care for the soil and extended ecosystems. Engaging "eco-ethical obligations," the dancers return the fungi to the forest. Once reestablished, the fungi care for the humans by providing nutrients, and sustaining the soil foodweb. "To properly care for the soil, humans cannot be only producers or consumers in the community of soil-making organisms but must work, and be, in relation with soil as a significant living world," affirms Bellacasa (2017, 202). In *Messengers Divinos* the dancers are in relation to the fungi (and by extension the soil), in reciprocal and nonreciprocal ways. In this way, Espinosa's choreographic techniques exemplify a practice grounded in a speculative ethics of care.

Mundane Actions

In *Messengers Divinos,* the haptic encounters of sight, sound, and touch/eat enable the dancers (and perhaps to some extent the audience) to "[engage] curiosity toward a web of doings, obligations, and asymmetrical reciprocities" (Bellacasa 2017, 199). This enacts a speculative ethics of care, as humans care for fungi, and fungi care for humans in the context of the foodweb. Writing about the eco-ethical obligations of performance, theatre scholar Wendy Arons asks, "How can we use live performance to honor our ethical and moral responsibility to, and interdependence with, the whole extant range of 'not nonpersons' – beyond just the human variety?" (2012, 569). This involves not just acknowledging their presence but also developing performance and dance practices, grounded in care and conscience, that collaborate with the more-than-human.

For Bellacasa eco-ethical obligations hinge on "modest changes" in everyday life "by creating mundane paths for our doings that acknowledge how we are already everyday companions" (2017, 199). Through the mundane actions of seeing, hearing, and touching/eating, *Messengers Divinos* demonstrates that humans are already entangled with other ecological matter, both in our creative practices and extended environments. Donald maintains that to embody the ethical ecological relationality of "Indigenous Métissage," "we must pay closer attention to the multiple ways our human sense of living together is constructed through the minutiae of day-to-day events, through the stories and interactions which always are imbued with a living principle of reciprocity, and hence moral responsibility for a shared future" (2009, 8–9). Ethical ecological relationality is concerned not only with everyday attunements to people, place, and ecological matter but also with the narratives humans create about these relations. Wilch argues that "performances like Espinosa's suggest a possibility that the environmentally concerned instead live differently, with sustained attention to our complicated interdependence and mutual fragility" (2020, 67). *Messengers Divinos* operates as both a narrative for living differently and praxis for creating performance/dance differently. How humans conceive of themselves within a relational web, like the foodweb, matters, whether it's in the context of performance or everyday life. For Bellacasa "an ethical reorganization of human-nonhuman relations is vital, but what this means in terms of caring obligations that could enact nonexploitative forms of togetherness cannot be imagined once [and] for all" (2017, 24). For humans situated in anthropocentric ontologies, the work of conceiving of nonexploitative ways of co-existing and embodying a speculative ethics of care is ongoing.

In this way, *Messengers Divinos* is not definitive, but rather, one thoughtful approach to a performance practice and choreographic technique that utilizes a speculative ethics of care to "enact nonexploitative forms of togetherness" in performance and everyday life (Bellacasa 2017, 24). Reconsidering approaches to care within the framework of performance, *Messengers Divinos* grapples with fungal/human relationships situated in Tsing's ruinous landscape (2015, 6) and Murphy's "alterlife" (2018, 118). *Messengers Divinos* uncovers life in the ruins by exhibiting the reciprocal and nonreciprocal relations among humans and fungi in the context of the soil foodweb. Espinosa's work offers a tangible example of the ways in which performance practices can experiment with "unexpected collaborations and combinations" (Haraway 2016, 4) to contend with trans-corporeal realities of "alterlife."

Notes

1 Hereafter referred to as *Messengers Divinos*.
2 The descriptions in this paper are based on the production I saw at the Houston Fringe Festival, and the online version from the Seattle Butoh Festival, which is available to view on YouTube.
3 For the Houston Fringe Festival (2018), Espinosa collaborated with Texas-based electronic musician DASHR to create the soundscape. For the Seattle Butoh Festival (2018), Espinosa collaborated with Washington-based electroacoustic artist Rocco Strain to create the soundscape.
4 Willie Crosby is the founder and director of the Fungi Ally mushroom farm. https://www.fungially.com/pages/about-us

References

Adamatzky, Andrew. 2022. "Language of Fungi Derived from Their Electrical Spiking Activity." *Royal Society Open Science* 9, no. 4:1–15.
Arons, Wendy. 2012. "Queer Ecology/Contemporary Plays." *Theatre Journal* 64, no. 4:565–582.
Baird, Bruce, and Rosemary Candelario. 2019. "Introduction: Dance Experience, Dance of Darkness, Global Butoh: The Evolution of a New Dance Form." In *The Routledge Companion to Butoh Performance*, edited by Bruce Baird and Rosemary Candelario, 1–22. New York: Routledge.
Bellacasa, María Puig de la. 2017. *Matters of Care*. Minneapolis: University of Minneapolis Press.
Donald, Dwayne Trevor. 2009. "Forts, Curriculum, and Indigenous Métissage: Imagining Decolonization of Aboriginal-Canadian Relations in Educational Contexts." *First Nations Perspectives* 2, no. 1:1–24.
Espinosa, Iván-Daniel. 2018. "A Skin That Sings: Movement, Mycelium, and Corporeal Choirs." *Caustic Frolic Interdisciplinary Journal*. Accessed October 6, 2023. https://causticfrolic.org/nonfiction/a-skin-that-sings/.
Espinosa, Iván-Daniel. Interview (virtual) by Angenette Spalink. Zoom. Bryan, Texas. July 8, 2020.
Fadel, Leila. 2022. "A new study suggests that mushrooms can communicate." "Morning Edition." *NPR*. April 7, 2022.
Fukasawa, Yu, Melanie Savoury, and Lynne Boddy. 2020. "Ecological Memory and Relocation Decisions in Fungal Mycelial Networks: Responses to Quantity and Location of New Resources." *The ISME Journal* 14, no. 2: 380–388.

Gagliano, Monica, Paco Calvo, Gustavo M. Souza, and Anthony Trewavas. 2020. "Plants Are Intelligent, Here's How." *Annals of Botany* 125, no. 1: 11–28.

Gibson, Prudence, and Catriona Sandilands. 2021. "Introduction: Plant Performance." *Performance Philosophy* 6, no. 2: 1–23.

Haraway, Donna J. 2016. *Staying with the Trouble*. Durham: Duke University Press.

Murphy, Michelle. 2017. "Alterlife and Decolonial Chemical Relations." *Cultural Anthropology* 32, no. 4: 494–503.

Murphy, Michelle. 2018. "Against Population, Towards Alterlife." In *Making Kin Not Population*, edited by Adele E. Clarke and Donna Haraway, 101–124. Cambridge: Prickly Paradigm Press.

Olsson, Stefan, and Bengt. S. Hansson. 1995. "Action Potential-Like Activity Found in Fungal Mycelia is Sensitive to Stimulation." *Naturwissenschaften* 82, no. 1: 30–31.

Program. *Messenger Divinos*. 2018. Houston: Mid Town Arts & Theatre Center.

Ryan, Courtney. 2013. "Playing with Plants." *Theatre Journal* 65, no. 3: 335–353.

Stamets, Paul. 2005. *Mycelium Running: How Mushrooms Can Help Save the World*. Berkeley: Ten Speed Press.

Tsing, Anna Lowenhaupt. 2015. *The Mushroom at the End of the World*. Princeton: Princeton University Press.

Wilch, Clara Margaret. 2020. "Embodying Climate Change: Self-Immolation and the Hope of No Escape." *Performance Research* 25, no. 2: 61–68.

Woynarski, Lisa. 2015. "A House of Weather and a Polar Bear Costume: Ecological Anthropomorphism in the Work of Fevered Sleep." *Performance Research* 20, no. 2: 24–32.

Woynarski, Lisa. 2020. *Ecodramaturgies: Theatre, Performance and Climate Change*. Switzerland: Palgrave Macmillan.

Conclusion
Moving with the Trouble

A transparent vertical chamber, about the size of a refrigerator, stands in the middle of a park. It is filled a quarter of the way with sand. A performer clad in beige shorts and a gas mask stands in the sand. Suddenly, blasts of air violently hurl the sand through the chamber, toppling the performer. The performer lies on their back with their feet in the air. The blasts cease and the performer slowly begins extricating themselves from the sand. They eventually stand up, sand visibly embedded in their hair and skin. The blasts commence again, sending them back to the ground. Sand propels through the air as the performer struggles, ostensibly "drowning" in the sand. The blasts conclude. The performer attempts to stand up. The blasts commence, again. The performer plunges toward the ground. This pattern continues indefinitely.

Correspondences (2021), an installation comprised of multiple sand-filled chambers, was conceived by multidisciplinary artist duo Ximena Garnica and Shige Moriya. It was performed by the LEIMAY Ensemble in Socrates Sculpture Park in Queens, New York.[1] Just as the biogeocultography of the bags of Fukushima dirt structured the movement of other bodies, so too does the sand's biogeocultography structure the movement of the human performers. Removed from its original geography and placed within transparent chambers, the sand is biologically altered and culturally reshaped as art. The violent motion of the sand launching through the air forcefully moves the performers by knocking them to the ground. It also irritates the performers' exposed bodies and makes it impossible for them to breathe without a gas mask. The choreography among humans and sand evokes trans-corporeal exchanges that biologically alter them both. The blasts of sand structure the performers' movements by toppling them, rendering them temporarily immobile. Once the blasts desist, however, the performers move. Even though they know the pattern of the sand blasts will continue, they do not remain permanently stationary. They attempt to extricate themselves from the sand, they try to stand. They keep moving, they persist.

As the sand moves the performers in forceful ways and impedes their breathing, it is hard not to read their enclosed environment as precarious, ruined, and harsh – the state of many global landscapes due to climate change,

Conclusion 97

extreme weather, and many other situated ecological "wicked problems." These harsh conditions embody anthropologist Anna Lowenhaupt Tsing's "global state of precarity" (2015, 6). Despite these devasting conditions, though, Tsing declares that we must continue "looking for life in the ruin" (2015, 6). And thus, the performers do so, they continue moving. They do not succumb to the bleak environment, rather, they keep going despite the calamitous mise-en-scène. Through their movement within the small transparent sand-filled chambers, they "stay with the trouble" (Haraway 2016, 1).

Multispecies feminist theorist Donna J. Haraway opens *Staying with the Trouble* (2016), by defining trouble: "It derives from a thirteenth-century French verb meaning 'to stir up,' 'to make cloudy,' 'to disturb" (2016, 1). It strikes me that movement is an integral component in each of these definitions. To stir up, make cloudy, and disturb, all involve an outside force moving an object or body. That is, something or someone enters a situation and purposefully or inadvertently moves a person or thing that alters the state of that situation. Trouble, understood as a verb (i.e., to stir up, make cloudy, or disturb), parallels, to a certain degree, performance studies scholar Dwight Conquergood's conception of performance as kinesis, "as movement, motion, fluidity, fluctuation, all those restless energies that transgress boundaries and trouble closure" (1995, 138). Movement, then, is a significant factor in disrupting, stirring up, and creating different modes of knowing and perceiving. It is therefore a latent (if not active) component of "staying with the trouble."

Understood through the theory of Haraway and Conquergood, the performers' choreographic responses in *Correspondences* are "staying with the trouble." That is, the precarious environment did not render them static. Through their movement, they persisted. They *moved* with the trouble. Haraway admits that "the horrors of the Anthropocene and the Capitalocene" make it challenging to not proclaim defeat, to feel that "it's too late, there's no sense trying to make anything any better" (2016, 3). She advocates, nonetheless, for humans to "stay with the trouble," and not succumb to indifference. She proposes that humans do this by "learning to be truly present… to live and die well with each other in a thick present" (2016, 1). In *Correspondences,* the performers are present in a "thick present." Confined to their performance spaces, they have no choice but to encounter the sand being expelled through the chamber. Through their perpetual presence and persistence, they *move* with the trouble.

If we need to *move* with the trouble. That is if we are to stir up, disturb, permeate, and transgress, we need to take movement seriously. That means thinking through the repercussions of movement, considering when we should move and when we should remain stationary. While movement can be hopeful, like the performers in *Correspondences* who persevere through the blasted landscape, movement can also have destructive and unintended consequences, such as displacement of peat which releases carbon into the atmosphere. Thus, moving with the trouble requires considering how movement, whether deliberate or inadvertent, structures the movements of other humans and more-than-humans. This also requires a consideration of the ways in which ecological "wicked problems" are issues of movement. If humans, in western epistemologies, approached these situated and multifaceted dilemmas through the framework of choreography, how could this disciplinary method reframe approaches to these problems? For example, examining deforestation through the lens of choreography focuses on the mass movement of trees involved in the process of clearing forests. The movements involved in these processes structure the movements of myriad others. Not only does the mass movement of trees damage habitats and diminish biodiversity, forcing humans, flora, and fauna to vacate their environments, it also impacts biosequestration and issues of food security, impacting access to breathable air and edible food. These intersecting impacts demonstrate the intricate embeddedness of biota and place, political, social, and economic systems. The choreography of one thing affects the choreography of infinite other things.

Considering the epoch's ecological crises through the framework of performance/dance offers different disciplinary perspectives and potentially generative approaches to moving with the trouble. As I demonstrate in this book by focusing on performances that examine the intersections of ecology and environmental racism (*The America Play*), extractive capitalism (*The Rite of Spring*), interactions of human and more-than-human bodies (*Las Mariposas*), and a speculative eco-ethics of care (*Messengers Divinos*), dance, and performance studies offer spaces to grapple with the hope and despair of the "wicked problems" of the Anthropocene.

Moving with the Trouble: A Return to the Beginning

> I pick up my right foot and place it on the muddy ground.
> SLLUUURRPP
> The mud sucks in my right foot, encasing it past my ankle.
> I feel cold water seep through my boot.
> I balance on my right foot and pick up my left foot and place it in front of me.
> SLLUUURRP
> The mud sucks in my left foot, encasing it past my ankle.
> I feel cold water seep through my boot.
> I balance on my left foot and pick up my right foot and place it in front of me.
> I continue in this rhythm
> Right
> SLLUUURRP
> Left
> SLLUUURRP
> Right

SLLUUURRP
Left
SLLUUURRP...

I tread alongside three botanists through a swampy, lowland forest in Virginia. At first the terrain feels overpowering, suctioning my feet and encasing my boots with thick, viscous mud. After a while, though, I develop a rhythm and my body adjusts to the way that the terrain has altered my movement. My physical movement through this geography inadvertently activates a biogeocultography. I biologically alter the forest as I compact the soil and deposit my sweat and skin cells. The forest also changes me, as vegetation and insects scratch and bite my skin, altering the invisible bacterial and fungal cultures that reside there. The embodied trans-corporeal exchanges among myself and the terrain alters us both. I leave parts of myself in the forest. Elements of the forest accompany me as I exit the space. These materials transform into abject objects as I attempt to remove them by washing the mud off my boots, scrubbing the dirt out of clothes, and picking the leaves out of my hair.

As this embodied experience in the lowland forest of Virginia demonstrates, the movement through one domain (e.g., geographical space) often results in unintentional movement through another (e.g., biological, cultural). My geographical movement through the forest has inadvertent biological and cultural repercussions. Thinking through biogeocultographic impacts can affect movement in everyday life – as evidenced by my botanical excursions – as well as dance and performance practices – as exhibited through the case studies in this book. Biogeocultography demonstrates that choreography is critical to the biological, geographical, and cultural meaning of ecological matter. When placed in a performance space, the biological, geographical, and cultural meanings of dirt, peat, and fungi are actualized and become vital performers. Ethical ecological relationality is not only about everyday attunements to humans and more-than-humans but also about the narratives and performances humans create about these relations. Moving with the trouble requires an ecological ethics of care. It requires thinking about webs of relationality and the ways in which humans and more-than-humans rely on reciprocal and nonreciprocal relations, in performance and everyday life.

Recognizing that dirt is often diminished, poet Sharon Olds begins "Ode to Dirt," with an apology: "Dear dirt, I am sorry I slighted you, I thought you were only the background for the leading characters—the plants and animals and human animals" (2021, 311). As this book demonstrates, dirt is not scenery for charismatic megafauna protagonists. It is vital performer and an active agent on stage. Olds concludes the poem with an invocation, "O dirt, help us find ways to serve your life, you who have brought us forth, and fed us, and who at the end will take us in and rotate with us, and wobble, and orbit" (2021, 311). Olds not only poetically alludes to the reciprocal and nonreciprocal ways that soil cares and sustains other life but also to the ways that movement is fundamental to the earth's soil. The organic matter and varied lifeforms that comprise the soil are in constant movement through the earth's rotation and orbit around the sun. *Choreographing Dirt* presents the diverse entanglements of materiality, movement, and performance, to demonstrate that the biogeocultography of dirt matters. By taking dirt and movement seriously, *Choreographing Dirt* offers a different perspective on the relationships among ecology, performance, and dance in the Anthropocene. It is my hope that the scholarly inquiries and performance practices examined in this book will enable our disciplines to continue to move with the trouble.

Note

1 This description is based on a October 22, 2021, recording of the performance, available on YouTube. For more information about the performance, see the artists website, https://socratessculpturepark.org/program/correspondences1/.

References

Conquergood, Dwight. 1995. "Of Caravans and Carnivals: Performance Studies in Motion." *TDR* 39, no. 4: 137–141.

Haraway, Donna J. 2016. *Staying with the Trouble: Making Kin in the Chthulucene*. Durham: Duke University Press.

Olds, Sharon. 2021. "Ode to Dirt." In *All We Can Save*, edited by Ayana Elizabeth Johnson and Katherine K. Wilkinson, 311. New York: One World.

Tsing, Anna Lowenhaupt. 2015. *The Mushroom at the End of the World*. Princeton: Princeton University Press.

Index

Page numbers in *italics* indicate a figure and followed by "n" indicate notes.

Abram, David 18n4; *Spell of the Sensuous: Perception and Language in a More-Than-Human World, The* (Abram) 18n4
Affect Theory 16, 17, 24, 25, 32, 33, 55, 58, 63, 64, 65, 66, 68, 69, 73; theories of *becoming* 58
African Burial Ground 24–25, 39n1
Ahmed, Sara 28, 30, 49
Alaimo, Stacy 5, 17, 58, 59, 66, 68, 73
Allsopp, Ric 13
Alvarez, Julia 17, 58–60, 71
Anthropocene 4, 7, 8, 9, 10, 12, 18, 37, 38, 97, 98, 100
Anthropocentrism 8–9, 12, 14, 16, 37, 51
anti-Blackness 38
Argentina's Dirty War 70, 75n7
Arons, Wendy 10, 11, 14, 93
Ashenburg, Katherine 6

Barbas-Rhoden, Laura 59, 69–70
Bardgett, Richard 5
Bausch, Pina 3, 17, 39, 42, 44–46, 55n3; *Gerbirge* 45; *Nelken* 45; *Rite of Spring, The* 3, 12, 17, 39, 42–43; adaptation 44; annual fertility rite 43; choreography 43; "Dirty" Dancing 48–51; extractive capitalism 98; history of 43–46; peat 46–48; performative taphonomy 54–55; Spring Demon Ritual 43; vital peat 51–53
becoming, 32, 33, 58, 62, ethics of 64–68, 74

Béjart, Maurice 44
Bellacasa, María Puig de la 62, 79, 83–84
biogeocultography 2, 16, 24, 35, 37, 42, 48; defined 2; of dirt transforms 73; of ecological matter 78; Foundling Father 39; of Fukushima dirt 3; neologism 2; trans-corporeal 73
bioperformativity 66–71, 78; of dirt 74
Black liberation and resistance 32
Blakey, Michael 23
Bogs 46–47
Borzik, Rolf 45
Braidotti, Rosi 68–69
Butoh 4, 18, 75, 78, 81, 82, 84–87; non-normative movement of Butoh 85

Callahan, Gerald 73
capitalism 10, 12, 13, 15, 17, 39, 54, 74, 78, 98
Capitalocene 10
Cass, Joan 43–44
Chakrabarty, Dipesh 9–10
Chaudhuri, Una 14, 17, 53; zoögeopathology 53–54
Choreographing Dirt 3, 5, 7, 12, 15, 18, 78, 100
choreography 2, 3, 11,12,13, 17, 18, 43–45, 52, 55, 58, 61–64, 69, 86, 88; 96, 98 ecological matter 13; of soil 16; of dirt 3,16,18,
Chthulucene 10
Climate chage 7–9, 11, 13, 17, 39, 47, 54, 96

Cody, Gabrielle 46
colonial capitalism 9
colonialism 8–10, 37, 83
coloniality 37
Conquergood, Dwight 38, 97
Correspondences (2021) 96–97
Cribbs, Shayna 63
Crist, Eileen 10
Croce, Arlene 48–51, 65
Crutzen, Paul 8
cultural performance 14
cyperaceae 4

dancers 17, 42, 48, 49–55, 58–71, 73, 78, 81, 82, 85–89, 92, 93: and fungi performing *79, 81, 91*; sacrifice 43–45
Deleuze, Gilles 16–17, 24, 35, 58, 63–65; *Thousand Plateaus, A* 64
deterritorialization 33, 65
dirt: bins of 58–62; biogeocultography 7; bioperformativity of 74; ; defined 2, 5, 62; and environmental racism 29–30; exchanges (Kaprow) 15–16; of Fukushima dirt 3; and human 62–66; *and Las Mariposas* (2010) 59–62; manifestation of labor 31; movement 3, 5; radioactive dirt 1–3, 6, 11; trans-corporeality of 74; transforms, biogeocultography of 73
dirtiness 7
"Dirty" Dancing 48–51
Donald, Dwayne Trevor 12, 79, 82
Douglas, Mary 2, 6, 30, 65
drama of disinterment 25
Dunnan, Nikki *61, 67*

ecocriticism 14, 59
ecodramaturgies 14, 19n10
ecological anthropomorphism 16
ecological relationality 82–84
ecology 3, 4, 7, 10, 12–16, 18, 84, 98, 100
Elam, Harry 36–37
enslavement 31, 37
environmental racism 12, 24, 29, 30, 32, 98
Espinosa, Iván-Daniel 3, 18, 78, 81–82, 88–90; *Messengers Divinos: A Meditation on Time, Space, Corporeality, & Consciousness* (2018) 3, 12, 18, 75, 78–79, 81–82; animals, plants, and fungi 79–80; Butoh and Mycelium 84–87; dancers and fungi performing *79, 81, 91*; ecocritical analyses 78; ecological relationality 82–84; haptic encounters 87–88; mundane actions 93–94; sight 88; sound 89–90; speculative eco-ethics of care 98; temporalities of care 82–84; touch/eat 91–92
Eveoke Dance Theatre 3, 17, 55, 58–59, 75n2
extractive capitalism 12, 98
extractive imperialism 37

Fischer-Lichte, Erika 43
foodweb model 7, 84, 86–88, 92–94
Foster, Susan Leigh 2, 11, 13, 27
Foundling Father 16, 24–29, 31–33, 36, 39, 48; deterritorialization 33–34; reterritorializatio 33–34
Fourteenth Amendment 31
Fourteenth of June Movement 59
Frank, Haike 25
Fukushima Daiichi Nuclear Power Plant 1, 18n1
Fukushima nuclear disaster 1, 18n2

Garnica, Ximena 96
Gawande, Atul 10
Gibson, Prudence 18n6, 80
global environmental change 8
Global Peatlands Initiative (GPI) 47
Golden Spikes 39n6
Gómez-Barris, Macarena 9–10, 59
Graham, Martha 44
Grice, Elizabeth A. 66
Guattari, Félix 16–17, 24, 35, 58, 63–64; *Thousand Plateaus, A* 64

Handschuh, Julia 13
Haraway, Donna J. 10, 74, 94, 97
Harrison, Rebecca L. 60
Henríque, José Manuel Marrero 59
Hernandez, Riccardo 26
Herz, Rachel 50
Hipchen, Emily 60
hooks, bell 32, 38
Hoskins, Te Kawehau 12, 51

Index 103

Houston Fringe Festival 81
humanity's relation with earth 70–71
human-soil relations 83
Hurt, Becky 63, 64, 69
Hutcheon, Linda 24, 35

industrial agriculture 47
Industrial Revolution 8
International Union for the Conservation of Nature (IUCN) 47
In the Time of the Butterflies (Alvarez) 17, 58

Johnson, E. Patrick 30, 31
Johnson, Kelli Lyon 60
Jones, Alison 51
Jooss, Kurt 44
Jordan, Winthrop D. 29

Kane, Adrian Taylor 59
Kanngieser, Anja 52, 55n6
Kaprow, Allan 15–16
Kazuo, Ohno 85
Kristeva, Julia 2, 50, 65

Laban, Rudolf 44
Larson, Jennifer 32
Las Mariposas (2010) 3, 12, 17, 55, 58–59; alterlife 71–75; bioperformativity 66–71; choreography 60; and dirt 59–62; dirt and human 62–66; staying with trouble 71–75; toxicity 71–75; transpositions 66–71
Lavery, Carl 3, 11
LEIMAY Ensemble 96
Lepecki, André 13
Le Sacre du Printemps see Rite of Spring, The (1975)
Lewis, Simon L. 8
Lincoln, Abraham 24, 32–33; assassination 33–34
Lindow Man 47–48
Liping, Yang 44
Lobell, Jarrett A. 46
Logan, William Bryant 5–6

Malone, Erika 60, 69
Manthropocene 10
Martin, Ronald E. 24
Maslin, Mark A. 8
Massine, Léonide. 44

materiality 12–13, 17; and movement 3, 64
May, Theresa J. 11, 14, 19n10, 48
McClintock, Anne 31
McKittrick, Katherine 23, 24
Megonigal, Patrick 2, 5
Miller, William Ian 50
Mirabal sisters 17, 60–62, 75n2, 75n8
Moore, Ericka Aisha 60, 65, 69,75n2
Moore, Jason 10
Moraga, Cherríe 70
Moriya, Shige 96
Morton, Timothy 15
Mount Holyoke Theatre 25
Murphy, Michelle 12, 74; Alterlife 71, 74, 79, 94
Mycelium 84–87

Nardi, James B. 5
New York City's La MaMa Experimental Theatre Club 81–82
Nijinsky, Vaslav 43

Ogden, James 26, 39n2
Orbis Spike 39n6

Palmer, Phyllis 7
papamihaw asiniy (flying rock) 82–83
Parks, Suzan-Lori 3,4, 16, 24–26, 35–39; *Death of the Last Black Man in the Whole Entire World, The* (1990) 25; *America Play, The* (1994) 3, 12, 16–17, 19n11, 23–27, 36–37, 48, 98; becoming Lincoln 32–35; ecology and environmental racism 98; movement generates meaning 27–32; putting the body back together 35–39; taphonomy 24; "Possession" 25; *Getting Mother's Body* 25; *Sinners' Place, The* 25; *Venus* (1996) 25
Patel, Samir S. 46
peat moss 17, 42, 45–55
performance 3–5, 11–16, 25, 42, 51, 58–60, 69, 71, 73–75, 78–80, 85, 90–94, 97–98
performance as kinesis 38, 97
performative taphonomy 16, 17, 25, 38, 39, 54, 71
Plantocene 10
Posthuman theory 12, 14, 66, 68, 73
Polyvinyl chloride (PVC) 71

racialization 28–29, 37
radioactive dirt 1–3, 6, 11; movement 3
Rayner, Alice 36–37
reciprocity of care 87
Ress, Mary Judith 59
reterritorialization 33, 65; of Black bodies 34
Riding, Alan 44
Rohman, Carrie 13
Ross, Anne 47

Sandilands, Catriona 18n6, 80
Seattle Butoh Festival 81
Simmons, Kali 37
skin 66
soil 5, 30–31; choreography of 16; defined 5–6; dislocation 2; organismal web 62; science 7; *see also* dirt
Solnit, Rebecca 6
sphagnum (*Sphagnum* L.) 46
Stacey, Jackie 49
Stamets, Paul 79, 80, 82, 84, 89
Stewart, Kathleen 33
Stoermer, Eugene 8
Stravinsky, Igor 43
Sundberg, Juanita 12–13

TallBear, Kim 55n5
taphonomy 16–17, 19n11, 23–27; becoming Lincoln 32–35; defined 24; movement generates meaning 27–32; putting the body back together 35–39
Tatsumi, Hijikata 85
Taylor, Diana 17, 58, 70, 71
Technocene 10

temporalities of care 82–84
Terbovich-Ridenhour, Molly 63–64
Todd, Zoe 9–10, 12–13, 52
trans-corporeal biogeocultography 73
trans-corporeality: 59, 73; of bodies 68, 71; of dirts 74
transpositions 66–71
Trujillo, Rafael 17, 59
Tsing, Anna Lowenhaupt 80, 97
Tuana, Nancy 53, 71

unearthing of bodies 23–24
Unearthing the Girls *61*

viscous porosity 53–54
Vital Peat 48

Wald, Sarah D. 59
Walker, Bruce 63
Warner, Sara L. 25
Watts, Vanessa 12, 17, 51
Wenders, Wim 42; *Pina* (Wenders) 42
Whitlock, Evangeline Rose 59, 63, 71
Whyte, Kyle Powys 9–10
Wigman, Mary 44
Wilson, Anastasia 27, 39n3
Wolfe, Cary 14, 73
Woynarski, Lisa 11, 14, 16, 27, 58, 69, 78, 88

Yale Repertory Theatre 26
Young, Vershawn Ashanti 31
yuck factor 49–50
Yusoff, Kathryn 9, 37

Zimring, Carl A. 30

For Product Safety Concerns and Information please contact our EU
representative GPSR@taylorandfrancis.com
Taylor & Francis Verlag GmbH, Kaufingerstraße 24, 80331 München, Germany

www.ingramcontent.com/pod-product-compliance
Lightning Source LLC
Chambersburg PA
CBHW051756230426
43670CB00012B/2312